KU-658-118

# THE PSYCHOLOGY AND
# TEACHING OF READING

A

# THE PSYCHOLOGY AND TEACHING OF READING

BY

FRED J. SCHONELL, M.A., Ph.D., D.Lit.

AUTHOR OF "BACKWARDNESS IN THE BASIC SUBJECTS," "DIAGNOSIS
OF INDIVIDUAL DIFFICULTIES IN ARITHMETIC," "ESSENTIALS
IN TEACHING AND TESTING OF SPELLING," ETC.

OLIVER AND BOYD LTD.
EDINBURGH AND LONDON
TORONTO: CLARKE, IRWIN & COMPANY LTD.

| | | | | |
|---|---|---|---|---|
| FIRST PUBLISHED | . | . | . | 1945 |
| REPRINTED | . | . | . | 1946 |
| SECOND EDITION | . | . | . | 1948 |
| REPRINTED | . | . | . | 1949 |
| THIRD EDITION | . | . | . | 1951 |
| REPRINTED | . | . | . | 1952 |
| REPRINTED | . | . | . | 1955 |

PRINTED IN GREAT BRITAIN BY
OLIVER AND BOYD LTD., EDINBURGH

# PREFACE

THE purpose of this little book on reading is to provide some information on what constitutes a scientific approach to the teaching of reading. During the past fifteen years there has been a considerable amount of well-planned and carefully executed research into many problems associated with learning to read, and it is vital that teachers and parents should be acquainted with the proven and pertinent points arising from this research. Possessed of such information, teachers and parents can establish adequate standards regarding the means and materials by which children are taught to read. Too long have children been handicapped by unsuitable reading methods and by unscientific textbooks. In not a few instances textbooks have been badly printed, with little attention paid to the development of eye-span as determined by size of print and adequate spacing between words and lines. Choice of illustrations for these same books has revealed both low educational and low æsthetic standards on the part of publisher and author. But perhaps the worst feature of some textbooks by which young children are expected to learn to read is the too heavy vocabulary burden employed. Words are not chosen from children's vocabularies, and for the less able 50 per cent. of pupils there are, in the early reading books, far too many new words per page. Informed parents and qualified teachers could do much to eliminate reading texts which show such blemishes as those cited above.

But more important than experimental findings on textbooks is the information now at our disposal concerning the early stages of reading instruction. Research shows that it is fatal to " push " young children along in the initial stages of learning to read, particularly if there have not been activities to create a functional language background beforehand. Most children fail in reading because they are plunged into formal reading with an over-analytic method employing abstract symbols before they really understand what words and sentences mean in spoken, let alone printed, form. Young immature minds need opportunity and time to "sort things out," to understand what they are doing, and to see the purpose in the operations with which they are confronted. My strongest plea in the teaching of reading is, don't hurry the children, don't expect too much in the early stages—do all you can to provide a language background. This slower, wider approach will repay doubly later on. The teaching of both reading and number would greatly benefit if we allowed children time to really understand and assimilate, indirectly and informally, at their own pace and through carefully planned experiences, the fundamental concepts in these two subjects, namely, the meaning of language and the meaning of numbers.

All pupils develop at different rates in different subjects. Only to-day I have examined an intelligent boy aged $10\frac{3}{4}$ whose arithmetic age is almost 12, but whose reading age is barely 8. The same kind of variations in development, particularly in reading, are to be found in infant classes, and we must be ready to provide for them. For this reason the *teaching* of reading should be conceived as a kind of unitary educational activity ranging over the years 5+ to 10+. The fact that pupils pass at 7+ from one department, or one class, to another should not lead us to think that all pupils should be taught to read in the infant school. Some children will learn to read in the infant school, others will not. This is not because the infant teachers have not worked sufficiently hard; in very many cases they do excellent work. My only wish is that some teachers would, particularly in early stages, do a little less " work " and allow their charges to proceed somewhat more leisurely and informally, and hence intelligently.

The pupils of 7+ who cannot read at the infant school

stage can learn to read at 8+ or 9+, or as late as 10+ in the junior school, *provided they receive suitable instruction and appropriate materials*. There should be complete dove-tailing between infant school or section and junior school or section in respect to these pupils who have not yet learned to read. The main objective of all teachers, in either department, should be to get all pupils to learn to read, and continuity is an essential factor in achieving this objective. Reading is of immense importance to the child's whole mental development. Apart from the obvious limitations that disability in reading imposes on progress in spelling, English, arithmetic, in fact in all subjects, it produces in most cases personality maladjustment, so that normal mental health cannot be maintained if there is failure in reading. Every child, except the lowest mentally defective cases and rare cases of cerebral lesion, can be taught to read. Teachers and parents should distrust the pseudo-psychologist who glibly labels children as word deaf or word blind, because he doesn't know why they fail to learn to read and to spell. Word blindness and word deafness are extremely rare conditions.

Certain backward readers require special scientific diagnosis of their conditions to discover their difficulties and to plan methods to overcome their handicaps, but in nearly all cases of reading disability this is a practical possibility, as I have shown in some detail in *Backwardness in the Basic Subjects*.

If teachers find that pupils are not making progress, they should do as much as they can within their power to find out why. Is the method right for this child? Is the material suitable? Don't let the child drift. Reading disability becomes increasingly difficult to treat the longer it persists. Similarly, parents should adopt the same enquiring yet not over-anxious attitude towards cases of backwardness in reading.

It is in this spirit that I offer to teachers and parents the

material set out in the body of this small book. In writing
it I have been impelled by a desire to inform them, to help
them, to give them hope, yet at the same time to lead them
to realise the immense importance of teaching every child
to read, and hence the necessity of making a scientific
approach to the whole problem.

F. J. S.

SWANSEA
1st *February* 1945

# CONTENTS

CHAP.                                                          PAGE

I. PSYCHOLOGICAL FACTORS IN LEARNING TO READ   .   .  11

II. PREPARATORY PERIOD IN LEARNING TO READ .   .   .  26

III. A PSYCHOLOGICAL ANALYSIS OF READING METHODS   .  44

IV. ORGANISATION OF READING IN INFANT CLASSES  .   .  66

V. ORGANISATION OF READING IN JUNIOR CLASSES   .   .  78

APPENDIX I. Graded Reading Vocabulary Test    .   .  92

APPENDIX II. Instructions for Giving, Scoring and Inter-
preting the Graded Reading Vocabulary Test    .   .  94

APPENDIX III. Suggestions for Compiling Exercises and
Work Cards or Work Books    .   .   .   .   .  100

APPENDIX IV. Exercises in Card Form based on the *Happy
Venture Readers* .   .   .   .   .   .   .   .  121

APPENDIX V. Methods and Materials for Backward Readers
in the Senior School  .   .   .   .   .   .   .  148

# CHAPTER I

# PSYCHOLOGICAL FACTORS IN LEARNING TO READ

MALCOLM, aged $4\frac{1}{2}$, is intrigued by a new game. It is the game of "reading." In his room he has three names printed in capital letters on separate pieces of cardboard, and he proudly informs one that he can read these words.

They are :  MALCOLM
PAT
BARRIE

A few questions soon show that he can "read" the names correctly no matter in what order the words are presented or in what form the questions are framed, as for example, "What is this one ?" or "Show me Barrie's name." How is it that a boy aged $4\frac{1}{2}$ can respond accurately to these printed words, although he does not know the names of more than two or three letters nor the sounds of any of the letters ? What are the factors which have produced this accurate discrimination of word patterns ?

In the first place it is obvious from our knowledge of Malcolm's acquaintance with letters and sounds that he is responding primarily to the total visual pattern of the whole word, and it is the marked difference in the visual patterns of the words which enables him to recognise each word. The length of the word and the nature of the letters which make up its visual pattern are the determinants in this discrimination. For example, his own name, MALCOLM, starts with M and finishes with M ; this gives it a certain discriminatory characteristic apart from its length. BARRIE finishes with E, a letter that Malcolm remembers from his attempts " to write " the name of his friend PETER, when he was told that E " has three arms, one long one at the top, a short one in the middle and a long one at the bottom."

11

Had Malcolm's name been JIM
and those of his friends TOM
and PAT it is quite possible that
he might not have shown the same facility and the same
degree of accuracy in his early " reading " reactions. The
fact that all the names would have been of similar visual
pattern would have made his task of recognition, *i.e.* of word
discrimination, much more difficult.

Now although distinctive visual pattern was the primary
means by which Malcolm recognised each of the three
words, yet we must remember that he had heard these
names many times and that they had maximum interest and
meaning for him. The words Barrie and Pat were symbolic
of all kinds of friendly social relationships and pleasant
play experiences. Furthermore, Malcolm had made several
attempts to copy his own name—imitative efforts more
nearly resembling drawing than writing, but nevertheless
helping him to recognise the visual pattern of the word
when he came across it in other places.

Thus we see that the factors which had contributed to
Malcolm's accurate " reading " or recognition of the three
printed words were fourfold—

    (*a*) the visual pattern of the words,
    (*b*) the saying and hearing of the words,
    (*c*) the meaning of the words,
    (*d*) the impressions gained through tracing or writing
        (or trying to write) the words.

Now of these four contributors towards word recognition,
the most important is the *visual pattern* of the word.

Every word has a distinct visual pattern produced by
its length and the nature of its component letters.

For example        all
                     one
                     eye
                     ate

are all of different pattern, although of the same length. But it is not as easy to distinguish them from each other as it is to distinguish them from longer words such as " said," " Fluff," " mother," " sixpence " and " elephant." Words in this latter group differ from each other both in length and in the number and position of the projecting letters of which they are composed. In word recognition more use is made of the projecting letters than of the lower-case letters, as is demonstrated in the following example, in which the first specimen is more easily read than the second.

(*a*) Thx pxxdxxtxxx xf pxppxt plxyx txkxx thx xdxx dxxxlxpxd xx thx pxxxxdxxg xhxptxx x xtxgx fxxthxx.

(*b*) x xurxxer exaxoraxion is xo xisxrixuxe xaxers anx craxons so xxax a xacxxrounx can xe maxe.
(A further elaboration is to distribute papers and crayons so that a background can be made.)

These basic facts of word discrimination are of extreme importance in the teaching of reading, for they have significant bearing on the selection of reading material, on the use of reading methods, on the causes of backwardness in reading, and on the use of effective reading material for backward readers.

Early reading material should contain common words of different visual patterns which will help the young reader in his difficult task of discrimination. If the material is overloaded with small words of similar pattern, such as ' an,' ' as,' ' on,' ' no,' ' or,' ' it,' ' at,' ' if,' ' of,' ' for,' ' by,' ' was,' ' saw,' ' are,' ' am,' ' hat,' ' hit,' ' boy,' ' big,' ' day,' the means of word recognition is decreased and the possibility of confusion is very greatly increased. All teachers are aware of the inability of less able pupils to distinguish ' on ' ' no '; ' of,' ' for '; ' was,' ' saw '; ' on,' ' in '; ' boy,' ' big '; ' day,' ' dig.' Yet many of these same backward readers can frequently recognise words like ' Fluff,' ' mother,' ' little ' and ' elephant.' It is in this aspect that the material of the average phonic reading book not infrequently presents unnecessary difficulties for pupils. For example, material such as the following,

> " The pig with a wig did a jig in the bog, *Phonic*
>    The fox saw a hen in the pen," *Difficu*

*eg*

although of regular phonic form, loses not a little of its advantage in this respect through the similarity of the visual patterns of the words employed,[1] so that some pupils read " pig " as " big," " bog " as " boy " or " big." This is a disadvantage apart from the obvious limitation imposed by the meaningless nature of the sentences.

Passing now from visual to auditory aspects of word recognition, we may note that saying and hearing words are essential factors in their later recognition. Although the nature and extent of the child's speech itself are important in the early stages of reading instruction, yet it is the more vital subtlety of the auditory elements of the words themselves that is gradually assimilated (very largely unconsciously) by the pupils through saying and hearing. Thus the pupil unconsciously understands that the word-sound PAT is derived from P-AT, and at a later stage he will be ready to realise (again unconsciously to a large degree) that it is like s-at, th-at, and c-at-ch. But in the beginning this knowledge is assimilated as an indirect and unconscious background for later usage.

Most children are not ready, either intellectually or experientially in English schools, at 5+ years, for an analytic-synthetic sound approach to reading. But at the

---

[1] This is not meant as an indictment of the phonic method of teaching reading, for it is recognised that without phonic knowledge of the right kind at the right time many children will not make satisfactory progress in reading. The advantages and disadvantages of various methods of teaching reading are considered fully in Chapter II.

same time much of the speech of the child, the saying of rhymes and other experiences of the preparatory reading stage are valuable indirect aids to the later phonic work which should be part of an intelligent reading scheme. It is because the hearing-saying aspect of word recognition is so essential in learning to read that young pupils should be allowed to say aloud or half aloud their reading material as long as they have the need for this aid.

Important as is the auditory-articulatory element in word recognition, it is subordinate to the influence of *meaning* upon the assimilation of words into the reading vocabularies of pupils. Recent psychological studies of reading have tended to emphasise the paramount value of meaningful material in both the preliminary and the instructional stages of learning to read. Words must mean ideas, not be merely mechanical patterns. Here we may note that the words which young children learn incidentally are those most meaningful to them." For example, one five-year-old could always read " ICE CREAM " wherever the word appeared. Furthermore, of the material in an introductory or pre-primer reading book, the words which pupils most quickly learn to read are those most meaningful to them ; words with least meaning are last to be assimilated into the reading vocabulary." The better and wider the background of the pupil's understood language the greater is his chance of success in learning to read, irrespective of other conditions. " Hence, learning to read must be preceded and accompanied by a background of language experiences obtained through home and school." Stories must be told and read, pictures must be shown and books provided so that a variety of talk about everyday situations will produce a wide vocabulary of common words. In this direction the school should plan boldly.[1] Activities for the five to six year-old stages should aim at building up that necessary background of language experience so vital to later work in reading, while vocabulary

[1] See *Play in the Infant School*, E. Boyce (Methuen).

extension and direct contact with word patterns, which appear in the pupils' reading material, should arise from the centres of interest of the six to seven year-old pupils. The keynote of the curriculum should be a constant attempt to expand vocabulary through language activities and real experiences; for the ideas produced by words are essential to normal attitudes towards word recognition. Conversely, of course, planned reading material for the first stages of reading from printed material should be related to the child's vocabulary. A recent study of the vocabularies of Scottish children [1] reveals the extent to which quite long words commonly occur in the speaking vocabularies of young children. Words such as 'always,' 'another,' 'auntie,' 'because,' 'clothes,' 'engine,' 'finger,' 'flower,' 'nothing,' 'penny,' 'people,' 'pictures,' 'porridge,' 'potatoes,' 'pudding,' 'sleeping,' 'something,' 'trousers,' 'writing' are very common. A comparison of the common words listed in this study with the vocabularies of certain infant readers [2] suggests that a considerable number of words common to the child's vocabulary are omitted, *i.e.* the material in some infant readers is not sufficiently based on child usage, and adult usage influences the content unduly.

Finally, the part contributed by *writing or tracing of words* towards their later recognition in reading should be carefully considered. As a supplementary means of revealing to pupils the function of words as indicators of real situations, and of acquainting them with varieties of word patterns, writing and tracing are essential experiences. Often the young child, having made or drawn a house or a harbour, a shop or a ship, a fort or a farm, wishes to label parts of

[1] *The Vocabularies of Scottish Five Year Old Children,* by A. C. and P. E. Vernon. Draft Copyright, 1943. The Scottish Council for Research in Education.

[2] *Word Counts of Infant Readers,* by A. C. and P. E. Vernon. Draft Copyright, 1940. The Scottish Council for Research in Education.

his model or his drawing—usually in the first instance it is merely to give a name to his total effort. Thus Malcolm would frequently come from his garden sandpen or his playroom with requests such as, " Will you write ' ship ' ? " or " How do you write (or spell) ' fort ' ? " These words would then be written on his drawings or copied by him on to separate labels of wood or cardboard and then put in conspicuous places on the models.

It is not too much to say that a considerable amount of early experience with word forms and word ideas can come through the drawing-writing or play-writing situations in a natural and therefore effective manner. The feel of the word to the child as he traces or writes it is of great value in cementing the visual and the auditory aspects of the words into a meaningful whole. The movement or kin-æsthetic impressions of words are no less important than the visual or the auditory impressions in learning to read.

## READING ABILITY

From the foregoing discussion of conditions influencing the basis of reading, *i.e.* word recognition, it is possible to enumerate the factors involved in reading ability. They may be listed as follows :—

(1) Level of general intelligence.
(2) Special mental abilities, namely, visual and auditory discrimination of word patterns.
(3) Experience and language background.
(4) Emotional attitudes of interest, individual application and confidence.

*These four sets of factors, mental and environmental, act interdependently to produce the composite power of reading ability.* We may then consider briefly the nature of each and the manner in which it operates to make its proportionate contribution to the complete ability of being able to read.

### (1) *Level of General Intelligence*

General intelligence is that inborn, all-round mental power which shows itself as an ability to see relationships between items of knowledge and then to apply these relationships to new situations. Level of general intelligence is one of the factors closely conditioning success in reading—obviously more intimately connected with power of understanding accurately and quickly what is read than with the level of word recognition. And while reading comprehension is to some extent dependent upon quick and accurate word recognition, both are examples of the perception and application of relationships. Thus the *mental age* of a child will be an important factor in determining, in some measure, the level and accuracy of his power of word recognition and of comprehension, while his *intelligence quotient* will indicate the speed of learning that can be expected from him. But the relationship between reading ability and degree of general intelligence is by no means absolute. There are not a few intelligent children who fail to make normal progress in reading, and numerous examples of rather dull pupils who can read quite fluently.[1]

All of these exceptions to the correlation between intelligence and reading ability can be explained by factors (2), (3) and (4) of the above classification. Nevertheless the mental age and the intelligence quotient are guides of considerable value to (*a*) the age at which formal reading lessons should be started with children, (*b*) the amount of progress that should be expected from them, and (*c*) the nature of the reading material that should be used with them. Mental age and intelligence quotient will be factors of importance in determining reading readiness. In the

[1] A striking example of this latter fact is provided by one residential school for mentally defective children where all pupils reach, before leaving at the age of 16, a minimum reading age of 11 years. This is achieved by the application of a scientifically planned reading programme.

past too little notice has been taken of mental age in the teaching of reading, and many pupils five to six chronologically, but only four to five mentally, have been doomed to failure by a too early start with the more formal aspects of reading. For really dull pupils it is not too much to say that indirect and preparatory stages of reading should be continued for as much as two years, *i.e.* until the children are at least seven years of age. The consensus of results from educational research indicates that for normal pupils the more formal approach to reading should not begin before a mental age of six is reached.[1]

## (2) *Special Mental Abilities of Visual and Auditory Discrimination of Word Patterns*

In addition to general intellectual power, ability in reading requires normal powers of perception in respect to the visual and the auditory patterns of words. These specific aptitudes, partly inborn, partly acquired, embrace firstly an ability to discriminate and to remember the visual patterns of words, and secondly an ability to associate sound units of words with the correct groups of letters— partly a breaking-down and partly a building-up process. Obviously, efficiency in these specific abilities is to some extent dependent upon normal powers of sight and hearing. Defects in either of these senses can cause acute reading deficiencies. But normal perceptual powers in the visual and auditory fields of word patterns mean more than normal sensory equipment. These particular perceptual abilities represent a *mental power which matures at different rates in different children.* This is evident from the cases of pupils whose intelligence, sensory powers, language background and emotional attitudes are normal, but who exhibit gross

[1] See C. A. Smith and M. Jensen, " Educational, Psychological and Physiological Factors in Reading Readiness," *Elementary School Journal* (1935), xxxvi, 583-594, 652-691.

reading disability in either the visual or the auditory perceptual fields.

These specific intellectual abilities are, in some degree, acquired, and one of the conditions which influences their development is early language experience.

Thus the discrimination of visual patterns of words can be aided by the nature of the reading approach, the material used and the form and layout of the print. A sensible approach which provides the pupil with contrasting visual patterns of words helps the growth of this discriminatory power and obviates early confusion which is likely to inhibit its development. It is clear, too, that early reading material which does not engender confidence through a relatively light burden of new words with adequate repetition might also prevent growth of normal visual perceptual power. (This, of course, excludes the preparatory reading stages when pupils are given liberal help in reading any sentences they dictate or associate with their play or projects.)

Furthermore, the nature of the print can aid visual perception. In the first introduction to a printed book the lines should be short, the type should not be less than 18 point and should resemble as nearly as possible the print script that the child is acquainted with in his writing. This can be achieved by use of an 18 point Gil Sans type. For example:

## Dora fell with the cat.
## The dog runs to Mother.[1]

In the first half of the first reading book one-line sentences are advisable; to begin with the child is confused if he has to carry on the meaning to a second line.

For later reading books the lines should gradually

[1] Taken from Introductory Book, " Happy Venture Readers," p. 10.

lengthen and the print should gradually decrease to 16 or 14 point, but finally should not be less than 12 point.

For example:

High in the house is a swing for the monkeys.[1]

"Stop, stop!" cried the clowns as they ran quickly after the ponies.[2]

Bold, clear type of correct size with adequate spacing between the words and between the lines is essential for correct discrimination of visual patterns of words. If the reader is at all doubtful of this, let him present a number of pupils, between the ages of 6+ and 8+, with type-written material to read, and then present similar material printed in suitable 14 point type. The increase in rapidity and accuracy of word recognition, particularly with the average and slow readers, is most marked. It is not only the size of the print that makes a difference, but the spacing between the letters, the words and the lines.

The question of spacing brings us to another important finding in the psychology of reading. Photographs of the eyes during reading show that the process consists of a series of eye movements and eye pauses. Nothing is read while the eyes are in motion, but only during the momentary pauses. The number and length of these pauses depends on the age of the reader and the difficulty of the material. Children make more movements and pauses in reading a line than do adults, and there is always a great increase in eye movements as the reading material increases in difficulty for particular reading ages. Thus, nine-year reading material given to a pupil of reading age seven greatly accentuates the

---

[1] (14 point). Book II, " Happy Venture Readers," p. 45.
[2] (12 point). Book IV, " Happy Venture Readers," p. 39.

amount of eye movements and the number of pauses in trying to recognise the difficult words. Hence the extreme importance of suitable reading material for children of differing *reading ages*—an objective that can only be achieved by effective sectional, group and individual reading within classes.

During each eye pause the reader fully recognises two or three words in the material being read, and partially recognises a word or two on either side. The amount properly recognised at one pause is called the *span of recognition*, thus :

## When they / got down, / they went / to see / the small / elephant.

The partial recognition on either side of the span of recognition serves two purposes ; it helps the child to recognise the next words and it aids his comprehension of what is being read.

If too many difficult words are introduced into the line of print, the span of recognition is unnecessarily narrowed, and as a result the ease and speed of reading, together with the amount of what is understood, are seriously hampered.

Thus, whereas the last example is suitable reading material for a reading age of 6 to 6½, the following would be too difficult :—

" One crane was unloading cases of butter from Australia " (reading age 7 to 7½).

Such material would seriously impede normal development of eye-span and accurate understanding. When material has to be " worried out " almost word by word, it is obvious that little can be understood of its content.[1]

One final point is the influence of the arrangement of

[1] In early reading books there should not be more than an average of two to three new words per page.

the printed material on the development of normal eye-span.
Plenty of eye-space surrounding lines, and words arranged
in possible " eye units " aid speedy recognition. Thus :

The children had tea.
"Now," said Dora,
   "let us play in a ring."
"Please hold my hand, Dora,"
said May.
"Hold my hand, Jack,"
said Dick. [1]

Here the arrangement of the material into useful
recognition units and the spacing at the beginnings and
ends of the lines make for rapid, clear perception and
hence for more effective eye movements.

Ability to associate sounds of letters or groups of letters
with their correct visual forms and to blend the sounds
into a complete word is, like power of visual discrimination,
a specific mental aptitude partly inborn, partly acquired. [2]
There is evidence to show that ability to distinguish the
visual patterns of words is easier than analysis and synthesis
of their auditory components. Both aptitudes mature at
different rates in different children, but the power of visual
differentiation matures the earlier. It is easier for the

[1] Taken from " Happy Venture Readers," Book II, p. 25 (Oliver and
Boyd Ltd.).

[2] For a full description of this specific factor see *Backwardness in the
Basic Subjects*, Chapter IX, Fred J. Schonell. (Oliver and Boyd Ltd.),
1942.

child to discriminate between the visual patterns of " Dick " and " Mother," " this " and " which," than it is for him to make a sound analysis of these words. At the same time as the child's reading vocabulary begins to increase he needs the specific power of sound analysis to help him with many new words—discrimination and memory of visual patterns is not sufficient. Thus he tackles numerous new words by a combined visual-auditory approach ; one can see this operating time and time again in the reading of pupils aged 7 to 8 years. For example, they meet the word " London " and quietly say L-on-don, at first calling it London (" o " as in " cot," not " o " as in " won ") and then rectifying any initial error in pronunciation. This analysis and synthesis occurs frequently with longer and newer words once the child has achieved a certain facility in reading.

Examples of words thus analysed into approximate phonic units that I have recently noted with one pupil of mental age $7\frac{1}{2}$ to 8 years are : " church, wanted, kinds, lemonade, sentences, dotted, to-morrow."

Thirdly, we come to essential environmental factors in reading ability, namely, language background and extent of experiences—the former dependent to a large extent on the latter. A variety of experiences, trips and visits, books and pictures, stories told and questions answered are all contributants to reading ability, for they furnish that background of spoken language so vital to an adequate meaning vocabulary. A child finds it easier to read words he has used frequently in his everyday life, and he finds it easier to understand reading material which deals with activities he himself has experienced. A background pregnant with meaning and experience provides clues to the nature of word patterns and enables pupils to make maximum use of context in word recognition.

Finally, there is the factor of emotional attitude in reading ability. We know now that the child learns best when he is eager to try and when he is interested. Some school methods produce these attitudes, others only imbue the child with a feeling of failure and frustration. Some parents, too, show a sensible attitude towards the child's reading problems by widening his experiences, praising his efforts, and not expecting unduly high standards in the early stages. Others do the opposite by limiting the child's opportunities, robbing him of confidence, or pushing him along too fast, ultimately into the abyss of confusion.

Parental attitudes and reading approaches which sustain interest, preserve confidence and foster the pupil's power of application and persistence make no mean contribution to progress in reading.

The material of the present chapter has revealed the complexity of the reading process and *the need for teaching methods to allow for gradual maturation in numerous directions, if success in reading is to be achieved*. Thus the nature of learning to read and the varying rates of development of different children in the factors producing reading ability make it imperative that there should be a properly planned preparatory period in learning to read. A detailed consideration of this preparatory reading stage will constitute the next chapter.

# CHAPTER II

## PREPARATORY PERIOD IN LEARNING TO READ

Most children come to school eager to learn to read, but too many of them lose this initial enthusiasm through early failure and discouragement. Why is this so ? The question can be completely answered in one sentence—because insufficient care is devoted to creating the correct type and amount of preparatory background for learning to read. As was shown in the previous chapter, reading is a complex process. Ability in it depends upon four major factors, each of which is characterised by a very wide range of development. This may be illustrated as shown on p. 27.

As has already been intimated, these factors act interdependently, so that a particular child may reveal all four characteristics highly developed and hence may be most favourably equipped for learning to read. A highly intelligent child, with a stable personality, whose perceptual powers are excellent and whose experiences and language background are exceptionally wide, usually learns to read irrespective of method or of the teacher's endeavours. But it will be apparent that there may be children who are ill-equipped in every one of the four named factors, or, if not in every one, then in at least two or three separate essentials. Imagine the pre-reading handicaps of dull children who come from very poor homes and who already show certain unfavourable emotional attitudes. What calamitous maladjustment must ensue from a too early start in formal reading (with its all too pointed, yet unavoidable, objective evaluations) with these children. With such a picture in mind it is impossible *that anyone should doubt the wisdom of a preparatory period in learning to read.* This is all the more urgent since, in English schools, children enter at the age of 5+ years. Evidence from my own researches shows that some entrants to infant classes are nearer 4+, and a few 3+, years in intellectual,

26

read

RANGE IN FACTORS DETERMINING READING ABILITY

| Factor. | Lower Limit. | Range. | Upper Limit. |
|---|---|---|---|
| 1. General Intelligence | Mentally defective. I.Q. 60–70 | | High grade supernormal. I.Q. 160 + |
| 2. Special Abilities. Perceptual power in the verbal field: (a) Visual (b) Auditory | Complete inability to discriminate simplest word patterns. Maximum confusion where visual or auditory elements are similar. Confusion of similar letters (b, d) or sound i.e. visual pattern (t, d). | | Highly developed visual and auditory power, so that pupil can often read and spell words of which he does not know the meaning. |
| 3. Experiences and Language Background | Extremely limited experiences and small vocabulary. | | Excellent meaning vocabulary and general knowledge through home discussions and various outdoor experiences. |
| 4. Emotional Attitudes | Completely unstable or lacking in initiative and independence; confused and lacking in confidence. | | Stable. Shows independence; can help himself. Persistent. Confident. |

experiential, verbal and/or emotional equipment. Hence it is imperative to consider our infant school pupils during their 5 to 6 years stage as being fitted out experientially and emotionally for the more serious demands of the 6 to 7 years' period. Provision for adequate maturation must be the keynote of the training in this first year—some dull pupils may even need a longer period for maturation, perhaps to 7+ or even 8+ years.

Now, in this respect, it is important to consider each pupil from an individual viewpoint. This can be accomplished by using some such guide as the reading readiness chart shown opposite.

It is suggested that this chart should be completed after the child has had several months in school. Any class teacher can find the mental age and I.Q. of each pupil from an appropriate *non-verbal test*, but she should accept a single I.Q. with caution. What she most requires at this age is an indication of the approximate intellectual power of the pupil, *i.e.* whether he is about I.Q. 80 or 95, about I.Q. 100, 110 or 120. Suitable tests are *Sleight Non-Verbal Test of Intelligence* (Harrap & Co.), and the *Moray House Picture Test* (U.L.P.). If time permits, the Terman-Merrill Test of Intelligence will give the most satisfactory result.

The chart has value not only from the material it yields about the children and the basis it provides for correct grouping later, but also because it brings more vividly before the mind of head teacher and class teacher alike the complexity of maturation needed for normal progress in reading. It shows that chronological age is much less important than mental age in determining readiness for reading; it shows that other factors besides either chronological or mental age exert an important influence. It emphasises the need to provide preparatory experiences of a wide and integrated kind which will enable consolidation to go on slowly and unconsciously through the first year at school.

*Read .*

## READING READINESS CHART

Name of Child .........................................................

Actual Age..................years..................months

1. Level of Intelligence.    Mental Age (M.A.) ...............
                             Intelligence Quotient (I.Q.) ......

2. Estimate of Experience Background.
   (a) (well above average)  (b) (above average)  (c) (average)
   (d) (below average)       (e) (well below average)
   Remarks :

3. Extent of play with other children.
        a        b        c        d        e
   Remarks :

4. Extent of vocabulary and talk with others
        a        b        c        d        e
   Remarks :

5. Any marked physical defects (sight, speech, hearing).
   Measures taken :

6. Observation of emotional attitudes.
   Recommendations.
   Future progress.

...............................................................

...............................................................

...............................................................

How is this background achieved ? What kinds of experiences should we provide for its effective development ?

## PRE-READING EXPERIENCES

The preliminary background for reading must be built up by providing the children with experiences that will lead to comparatively rich and varied language development. (1) Their spoken language must be wide enough to cover many of the common words and ideas that they will later meet in a printed form. Without such a background of spoken language there is a chance that the printed symbols will have only an artificial and arbitrary meaning for some pupils. (2) Furthermore, the indirect experiences of the pupils with books, pictures and printed words in different situations should be such as to create the correct attitude towards reading. The printed word must " tell something " to the child ; it must unfold information that he likes to hear, that provides pleasure and incentive for him.

The preparatory reading stage may be divided into two periods—

(a) that between 3 + and 5 years, spent either entirely at home or partly at home and partly in a nursery class or nursery school ;

(b) that between 5 and 6 years of age, spent in an infant class.

(1) In both periods play will be the most profitable activity for the development of language. In the former period a variety of materials and toys should be provided so that situations will develop which demand the use of language. Naturally such situations will most likely arise in a well-ordered nursery class. Here the pupil will have the added incentive to talk and to indulge in dramatic play through constant contact with other children. This early play period is regarded by many psychologists as indispensable

to the pupil's later application in school activities. Certainly it enables the child to try out his emotional self and gradually to stabilise himself through expression of his emotions in a variety of situations. Charlotte Bühler [1] has produced evidence that the pupils who fail in their play, either through some environmental limitation or from some early emotional maladjustment, are not infrequently the ones destined to become failures in school.

In this period, too, the use of picture books and pictures with simple captions will do much to mould the initial stages of an understanding attitude towards books. [2] Particularly useful is the child's attempts at drawing and painting for clarifying his conceptions of everyday experiences —a considerable amount of speech often derives spontaneously from the child's artistic efforts, which represent a desire to show what he knows rather than what he sees.

But just as valuable as the play of the 3 to 5 period is the contact with understanding adults. The young child is doubly fortunate if he finds these in both his school and his home. It is in this way that the much discussed only child often makes up very much more by this contact than he loses in the lack of child companionship. Intelligent parents—and contacts with other interesting adults—can produce most amazing vocabulary development in young children, and it is not an exaggeration to say that normally intelligent children under such conditions may often, in vocabulary, be two or three years ahead of other children of the same age in a less fortunate environment. The constant and varied discussion that naturally arises in many one-child families provides for unlimited vocabulary development on the part of the child.

[1] See *Birth to Maturity* by C. Bühler.

[2] The various materials and associated play situations for this stage are admirably described in *The Child under Eight*, vols. i-iv, ed. by F. I. Serjeant (Gresham Publishing Co.), and also in *Learning and Teaching in the Infant School*, Chapter IJ, by E. G. Hume (Longman & Co.).

Even more useful than the informal discussion with adults are the stories read and told to children. Here, of course, nursery classes can make this provision for all children. A considerable amount of speech and questioning can arise naturally from story situations.

Although by far the greater amount of the preparation for reading in this first period (3 to 5 years) is general in nature and entirely incidental, yet there are occasions upon which children can be helped to discriminate their own name from others. There are times, too, when they request one to write the name of a favourite friend or animal, or to provide a name or a title for their constructive efforts. These and other such sporadic examples should be fostered, for in them lie the very beginnings of successful word recognition.

## PREPARATORY STAGE (SECOND PERIOD, AGE 5-6 YEARS)

Perhaps one of the most natural and most effective ways of introducing pupils to the reading situation in this second preparatory stage is through their growing interest in drawing and painting.[1] At 5+ the child is beginning to use his brush, crayon or pencil with sufficient co-ordination to show what he knows about everyday situations and activities. Usually he wishes to talk about his drawings, and this natural connection between speech and action may be used to start a real interest in writing and reading.

For pupils at this age a simple drawing book can be made by sewing into a semi-stiff paper cover a number of

[1] Some of the ideas in this section I owe to the co-operation with Miss F. I. Serjeant, Lecturer in Infant Method, Goldsmiths' College, University of London. Miss Serjeant's insistence upon the psychological need for an adequate period of preparation in the pre-reading period, based on use of the pupil's everyday interests, has made a useful contribution to the teaching of reading in English schools.

paper butts (4 inches long and 1 inch wide) to which blank drawing pages can be pasted.

The pupil draws, in colours, anything he likes (usually something relating to home, play, or everyday experiences) and then the teacher, at the pupil's direction, prints a

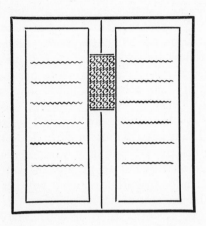

DAPHNE'S

BOOK

number of sentences on the opposite page. A specimen of a page from Malcolm's book (at age 5½ years) is given on pp. 36-37.

The teacher reads the page over to the pupil, who then tries to repeat the sentences with very liberal help. _No standard is fixed and no attempt at formal correctness is made in this work, but indirectly a meaningful reading situation is created._ Later the pupil may trace over the sentences with a crayon or a thick black pencil, a prelude to a further step of copying sentences. In this way writing and reading situations are naturally linked. Sometimes the pupil cuts out and pastes into his book pictures about which rhymes may be written. What has been printed by the teacher has maximum meaning and interest for the pupils—essential requisites in learning to read.

## CONSTRUCTIVE AND MAKE-BELIEVE PLAY

In addition to drawing and painting, pupils of 5+ should be allowed to pursue individual interests connected with making things and arranging materials. A variety of odds and ends such as wood (*e.g.* suitably sawn to represent the hulls of boats, or in various shaped blocks), clay, cloth, boxes of all sizes, paste and paints should be provided.[1] Pupils may be given a little guidance in this work, but for the most part they will follow individual desires and make something which satisfies them—it is only with pasting, pinning, nailing or painting that some assistance may be required. Together with making things, children like arranging materials such as boxes (to make " play " boats, houses, lifts, forts), small animals (to put in farmyards or zoos), soldiers, trucks, guns (to set out in encampments), tiny aeroplanes, hangars, searchlights (to arrange in aerodromes), small ships (to arrange in harbours or on voyages), trains, trucks (to arrange on lines or in lines).

Associated with all these activities there is considerable talk and some questioning. More advanced pupils often require labels to be printed so that they can place them on what they have constructed or what they have arranged. All this individual or small group work is a natural preparation for a group study or centre of interest which may be successfully planned with 5½ to 7 year olds.

## GROUP STUDY OR CENTRE OF INTEREST

A sound reading programme aims at teaching pupils to read in a way that is meaningful and satisfying. Actual contact with printed symbols should be preceded by and

---

[1] The teacher will derive considerable help from *School Activities and Equipment*, by Rose B. Knox (Houghton Mifflin Co.), and *The Activities Curriculum in the Primary Grades*, by Marion P. Stevens (D. C. Heath & Co.).

accompanied by experiences which really interest children and which ensure that they understand what they read. The idea should be constantly kept in mind that children will recognise words more easily if the material to be read represents pleasant actions and experiences with which they are familiar. Thus reading material should be intimately related to the children's lives. To achieve these various aims the obvious method of approach is to relate early reading matter to a group study or centre of interest in which all pupils are interested and in which all can participate.

Practically every child is interested in building a house, and if a suitable space in the classroom is available this is an activity which can be linked with much meaningful reading.[1]

According to the age of the pupils there will be proportionate limitations to their building efforts; pupils of 6+ are much more effective in planning and in making continuous efforts than pupils of 5+ years. If possible, younger children may be aided by providing large cardboard boxes, which can be slit along certain sides to provide a house with ceilings and rooms, and then various aspects of decoration may be pursued from that point. But what is enjoyed best is the building of a house from the beginning, so to speak. For this purpose the teacher provides a couple of clothes horses, or trestles with laths to form the walls of the rooms. Then all pupils paint patterns or pictures on large sheets of paper which are pinned on to the frame of the walls. All-over patterns may be made by older pupils to form quite attractive walls.

Talk about the home and those who live in it may keep pace with the building of it. Reading sheets may be prepared by the teacher using simple words and dealing with the interesting aspects of the home as they develop. Thus, initial talks may centre round Mother and Father and

[1] Other studies suitable for the $5\frac{1}{2}$ to 7 year period are making shops of different kinds, preparing for and giving a party, etc.

The engine is going
to Scotland.
The coal is in the truck
The coal is going to
Scotland.

(Malcolm had twice been by train to Scotland.)

about a boy and a girl named Dick and Dora who live in the home.

The first reading sheet may show :

> Mother lives in this home.
> Father lives in this home.
> Dick lives in this home.
> Dora lives in this home.

In further talks the pupils may suggest that Dick has a dog and Dora a cat. The pupils may then make a drawing of Dick's dog and Dora's cat. The names of Nip and Fluff may be selected for these animals. A further stage in the compilation of the reading sheets may include

> Dick has a dog.
> Dora has a cat.
> Dick's dog is called Nip.
> Dora's cat is called Fluff.

The teacher may read these sentences through to the class and then the class read them through with her. In addition some of the brighter pupils may be encouraged to read the sentences individually. Here again there is no formal teaching as such. Some pupils learn some words, whilst brighter ones may even assimilate quite a number of common words.

The next step in the building of the house is the attractive one of interior furnishing and decoration  Boxes are used to make a table, chairs and cupboards. This involves some sawing, hammering and painting by the boys. At the same time the girls may be encouraged to sew with brightly coloured wools or beads dish-cloths to make curtains for the windows and cupboards.

Then some pupils make table-cloths from paper, cut out in patterns or coloured with crayons or paints, while others make coloured table-mats from stiff paper.

The making of utensils—cups, saucers, plates—is usually a fascinating part of the study, and here papier mâché is suitable ; it can be hardened and covered with white paper upon which simple patterns may be painted. Knives, forks and spoons are cut from stiff paper or cardboard. Imitation foods may be prepared by mixing flour and salt (3 parts flour to 1 part salt) and then allowing pupils to mould loaves of bread, cakes, eggs, fruit, etc. The salt causes these to dry hard, after which they may be painted or covered with coloured paper or tinsel such as is found around chocolate biscuits.[1]

In addition it is possible to develop all kinds of interior decoration such as construction of vases (from flour and salt covered with brightly coloured paper), drawing pictures illustrating stories told by the teacher, and making toys (balls, tops, cars, boats) to be placed in or near the home.

A useful preparation for word recognition is the use of labels both on the various parts of the house and on its contents. These are of inestimable help later, as in the more systematic stage of learning to read the pupils will be reading about their activities connected with the home, and many of these words will appear in the printed material.

Coincident with the building and decorating of the home and the making of articles for it, the teacher may continue stories about the activities within the home by its different occupants. She will relate what Nip can do— beg for a bone, play with a ball, play with Dora and Dick— and she will encourage pupils to discuss what Fluff does —where she sleeps, what she eats and all about her kittens. Stories will be told about Dora and her doll Jane, Dick and Dora, Nip and Fluff playing hide-and-seek, about skipping and jumping, about visits to the shops and about tea in the home.[2]

---

[1] Obviously under conditions of food rationing the flour and salt mixture cannot be used. Plasticene may be substituted.

[2] This discussion will form an excellent background of meaning and vocabulary when pupils are introduced to Introductory Book (*Nip and Fluff* ) and Book I (*Playtime*) of the Happy Venture Series.

Only a few of the incidents connected with building and furnishing the home and occasional stories told by the teacher will be used for the reading charts [1]—not a little of the material will be for extending experiences and increasing vocabulary preparatory to the more intensive teaching of reading.

At the same time the more able children (mental age 6 + onwards) can make good use of the reading sheets to assimilate common words, many of which will appear in their first readers.

Supplementary to the reading sheets are the reading books which the pupils can prepare for themselves. These are similar to those described in an earlier section, but deal specifically with the group study and the people (Mother, Father, Dick, Dora, Nip and Fluff) connected with it.

Older pupils of 6 + may be expected to make use of work books. These contain cyclostyled sheets, previously prepared by the teacher, and consisting of simple sentences relating to the group study. The sentences are formed of words which will appear in the first reader and they all involve drawing, colouring, cutting-out and pasting. Examples of pages from a teacher-made work book are given elsewhere.

Other exercises which can be used to extend the reading value of the group study are

(a) matching cards,

(b) copying sentences from the blackboard.

(a) Cards such as the Happy Venture Reading Cards (Oliver and Boyd Ltd.) may be used, and sets of words given to each

[1] The amount of material used by the teacher for reading sheets or for the pupils' work books, the level of construction in the group study and the amount of word recognition and assimilation will depend much upon the age and calibre of the children. Varying standards and varying contributions will be expected from different children within the same age group.

pupil. The simple sentences on the card are then matched by the pupils from the separate words.[1]

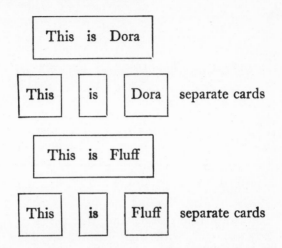

(b) More able pupils of 6+ who have made some progress with writing may be allowed to copy a sentence relating to the group study from the blackboard.

### SIMPLE SUPPLEMENTARY READING DEVICES

Simple supplementary reading devices for this pre-paratory period should be given a place in the daily time-table. Thus a library table on which are coloured pictures with simple captions, good picture books which the children will want read to them, and collections of cards bearing pictures and rhymes will contribute towards satisfactory reading readiness.

The keeping of a nature calendar, a weather-chart and a news-sheet, all provide opportunity for contact with

[1] The Happy Venture Matching Cards provide graded material for matching words, phrases and sentences found in the *Happy Venture Readers* (Oliver and Boyd). See Appendix IV, p. 121.

meaningful printed material relating to the pupils' own experiences.

*E.g.*

| Monday | wet | Monday | Fed the tadpoles |
|--------|-----|--------|------------------|
| Tuesday | fine, cold | Tuesday | Tom brought a newt |
| Wednesday | fine, windy | Wednesday | Went into the woods |
| Thursday | dull | Thursday | |
| Friday | cold | Friday | |

Pupils of 5½ can be led to keep a simple chart such as the above. Further verbal influences may be arranged through the use of labels associating the names of fruits, vegetables, seasons, etc., with their printed symbols. Activity cards are useful with the older and more able pupils :

> Clap your hands.
> Shut the door.

Nursery rhyme cards with appropriate pictures are also helpful at this age.[1]

## RESULTS OF THE PREPARATORY STAGE

The results of this preparatory reading period between the ages of 5½ and 6 years, or beyond 6+ for some pupils, should have been firstly to provide the pupil with the necessary experiences and to stimulate his talk so that he will acquire a vocabulary helpful in his understanding of the printed words. Secondly, this period should arrange experiences intimately associated with the child's life which

[1] For detailed considerations of these and other devices see *The Child under Eight*, ed. by F. I. Serjeant, pp. 10-27 (Gresham Publishing Company).

can form the basis of his reading material. If he has made the things, talked about the experiences and seen words associated with the activities and objects on which his first reading books are based, he is likely to succeed in the all-important task of learning to read. Finally, with respect to this period, and as a preparation for the second, more formal aspect of learning to read, teachers should note that little is achieved by forcing pupils to read. Many of them will make little apparent progress between the ages of 5 and 6, then in the 6+ stage they will forge ahead with rapid strides. In this preparatory period give them all kinds of opportunities for achieving the necessary verbal background and the right attitude towards words, but do not set rigid standards. The consolidating period between 5+ and 6 or 6+ is often not measurable ; its effect is often delayed, but there is little doubt of its value from 6+ onwards for those children who are fortunate enough to have had it.

# CHAPTER III

# A PSYCHOLOGICAL ANALYSIS OF READING METHODS

FROM the flexible preparatory reading stage described in the last chapter we now pass to the more systematic reading lessons which should take place in an intensive way with pupils of *mental* age 6+ onwards. Naturally not all pupils in a 6 to 7 age group will be ready for the more formal introduction to a reading book, and for those not ready a continuation of methods such as outlined in the last chapter is probably the best procedure. For the others the problem of method needs consideration, and this seems a suitable point at which to consider methods of teaching reading as such. Briefly, we can enumerate three methods of teaching reading :

(*a*) the phonic method,
(*b*) the word whole or " look and say " method,
(*c*) the sentence method.

Although we may consider these as separate methods, it is not very often that we find only one method used for a continuous period to teach pupils to read—perhaps the only example would be a thorough-going phonic method. Actually the main interest lies in the answer to the question, " Which method is used in commencing to teach reading ? " ; for most enlightened teachers make their reading method (after a time) a combination of all three methods.

## (*a*) THE PHONIC METHOD

This is an analytic method which aims at providing pupils with the sounds of the various letters of the alphabet.

By various picture and letter association devices the pupils
are taught that

a says a    as in *a*pple
b  „  b    „  „  *b*at
c  „  c    „  „  *c*at   and so on.

Then they are given regular words to read.

Only one sound is given for each letter, so that the
scheme is weak in the first place because it provides only
26 sounds out of the 60-odd sounds which the 26 letters
of the alphabet may represent.[1] For example, *a* may be
sounded as in " c*a*t," " *a*ll," " *a*te," " *a*rm " or " *a*ny."
Using only one sound form of each letter limits to some
extent the reading material that can be used in first reading
books. Irregular words (here, one, Mother) must be
omitted or else learnt as word wholes. Furthermore, words
containing the vowels must be of the five taught forms—

---

[1] There have been attempts, happily now no longer used, to provide
phonic alphabets, in which the variations in sound of the vowels, the
silent letters and the several sounds of some consonants have been
indicated by particular marks on the letters themselves. Of such a
kind was the Hayes phonoscript method. In Hayes phonoscript primers
special distinguishing marks were put on the various variations of the
vowels and consonants. Thus :

> *a* as in " cat " was printed without any mark,
> *a* as in " all " had a mark in the middle of the letter,
> *a* as in " cage " had a mark at the base of the letter.

Then there would be lines of print giving practice in these modifications
of the sounds, *e.g.*

> Paul has a pet cat.
> Paul's train is all bent. He will weep.   (ee and e would have
> Let me tell Sam.                          distinguishing marks.)
> Pip is a gentle little pet.
> It has a cage.

All final letters which were not sounded had a " silence " mark. See
*Phonoscript Primer* by Alfred E. Hayes (G. P. Putnam's and Sons Ltd.,
London), 1922.

*a* as in " c*a*t," *e* as in " w*e*t," *i* as in " b*i*t," *o* as in " c*o*t," *u* as in " c*u*t." Obviously these limitations make the reading material largely artificial. Thus in one phonic reader we find :

> The red hen is in the pen.
> The pig in a wig did a jig.
> The wig fell in a bog.

Such material is not related to the pupil's interests, activities and everyday experiences, and can have little real attraction for them. No preliminary background of vocabulary and understanding are created by the advocates of this method.

Another disadvantage of the limitation in word forms available for phonic readers is that too many two- and three-letter words are used. As a result of this, pupils are not only deprived of the most important means of learning words, namely, through contrast of their visual patterns, but confusion of words of similar length (' on,' ' no '; ' as,' ' in '; ' is,' ' so,' ' if,' ' of,' ' for,' ' was '; ' saw '; ' am,' ' an ') is thereby produced. There is insufficient use of longer common everyday words like ' Mother,' ' Fluff,' ' bring,' ' this,' ' play ' to form contrasts to words like ' on,' ' is,' ' at,' ' to,' which should be very sparingly introduced at properly spaced intervals into early reading material. Moreover, numbers of small words with artificial association destroys the story element which means so much to young pupils.

Psychological research confirms the opinion that for many pupils the phonic method is too analytic—they do not really understand what they are doing, and not a few of them are mentally unable to associate sounds with symbols and then to analyse and blend these as they find them in words. Dolch and Bloomster [1] provide evidence that few children

[1] E. W. Dolch and M. Bloomster, " Phonic Readiness," *Elementary School Journal* (1937), xxxviii, 201-205.

with mental ages below seven show ability in phonic analysis, even where there has been systematic instruction. My own experience is that it is not until about *mental age 7* (*i.e.* pupils of 6+ years of above average intelligence) that a child can intelligently make extensive use of the breaking-down-building-up method of tackling new words.

A further disadvantage of the accompanying analysis and synthesis of the phonic method is that it tends to slow down learning by word wholes, and hence interferes with the idea of grasping words, phrases and sentences as meaningful reading units. This is particularly so where drills on groups of similar phonic words are excessive. With some children sounding becomes an end in itself, and in consequence both normal eye movements and understanding of what is read are unnecessarily impeded.

One advantage of the phonic method is that it gives the pupil more power in tackling *certain new* words, not, as is claimed, a method of tackling *many* new words, for irregular words must be learnt as wholes; variations from the learnt vowel and consonant sounds occasion difficulty to all but the bright pupils. However, this confidence produced in pupils by the use of simple controlled material in the initial stages is not to be underestimated. My own experience is that I would rather see children of below average intelligence using a phonic method than an ultra-modern " experience " or " project " method where the material is simply " groaning " with a too heavy vocabulary burden which does not give the pupils a chance to learn gradually a selected number of new words. Such a method is all project and little reading. Actually neither method is the most effective with the duller section of the class.

It is obvious from the foregoing remarks that the phonic method for *beginning* reading is not the most suitable approach. This fact is being increasingly recognised by intelligent teachers. But it is also just as sure that at a certain stage in the pupil's reading he requires some phonic training, and that he is held up if it is denied him. To this point I shall return later in the chapter when the place of phonic training in a sensible reading programme is discussed in detail.

Some teachers, while following a phonic method, use the word whole method in conjunction with it. Irregular words are put at the top of each reading page and pupils learn these before commencing the lesson. This does reduce the artificiality of the reading material, but on the whole the method labours under the various disadvantages previously outlined.

### (b) THE WORD WHOLE OR "LOOK AND SAY" METHOD

As the name implies this method of teaching reading commences with a unit larger than the letter or sound, namely, the word. To a degree this method is psychologically sound, for it starts with large meaningful units which the child understands as "telling him something" and which provides for easier discrimination through length and shape of differing word patterns (see Chapter I). The method is sound in so far as words like "run," "jump," "dog" may assume for a young child the nature of a complete language unit, *i.e.* the word may be equivalent to the true unit, a sentence, for the above words may mean "See me run," "I can jump," "Here is my dog." In this respect much more meaningful material is employed early in this method of teaching reading than in the phonic method. Furthermore, words are soon expanded into sentences. Some teachers introduce the word whole method through an extensive use of pictures. Cards are prepared which have a picture illustrating the word or revealing its meaning with the word printed underneath.

| Run | Jump | Tom |
|-----|------|-----|

(1) Meaningful material

Then the next development is short sentences :

> Run to Tom.
> Jump to Tom.
> Tom jumps.
> Tom runs.

A limitation of the method is that it does not always rest on that secure foundation of pre-reading preparation which characterises the sentence method. Pupils are sometimes deprived too long of the very real aid of contextual clues as conveyed by the sentence, and therefore a too long initial introduction through words alone may set up a considerable amount of guessing. However, progressive teachers, who make full use of pictures and activity work and who soon merge words into sentences, obtain striking success with this method. My own experience is that *the word whole method of commencing reading, particularly when concrete words adaptable to illustrations are used is the best method to use with the duller 25 per cent. of the class.* A small vocabulary based on the children's interests can be built up very quickly.

## (c) THE SENTENCE METHOD

In the sentence method of teaching reading the sentence is regarded as the unit to which the pupil is introduced. In its early form the sentence method was artificial and psychologically unsound—the sentences used were unrelated to children's interests and activities and were too long and difficult. Not a few pupils were destined to failure when the early material was of this type :

" The round moon is shining on the silvery water."

Pupils were acquainted with the sentence through a short story and a picture. Further sentences and pictures about unrelated topics, followed by sentence matching or word matching often completed the confusion of the poorer members of the class.

Some of the most backward readers I have had to examine during the past ten years were rather dull children who had been taught by this artificial kind of sentence method. This form of sentence method has happily disappeared, and in recent years the method has been linked with the real experiences of the children. As a result the sentences have been real and natural. Moreover, sound textbooks have limited the sentences to three or four words in the initial stages. To begin with, short sentences like these are used :

> This is Dick.
> This is Nip.

Then two or three sentences about Dick and Nip may follow, and next a simple story of four or six lines embodying some incident. Later sentences lengthen to seven or eight words, repetition being used to help the development of word discrimination.

On page 51 is reproduced a page from a textbook based on a scientifically planned sentence method approach, with small vocabulary burden and illustrations of maximum assistance to the pupils.

The great value of the sentence method lies in the help it offers to the pupil from the context and from the continuity of meaning that can be embodied in the material. Although sentences appear as the units, all pupils have had some association with many of the words used during the preparatory stage (see Chapter II), because the method is based on child experiences and activities, and hence makes use of everyday words that the child uses in those activities. It is not restricted in its words or material, and its selection of these is psychologically sound for it is based on child development. In the centre of interest previously outlined many pupils have had experience of words like " Dick

Dora will wash Jane.
  She is a rag doll,
  so Dora can wash her.
Dora has a line by the tree.
May sits on a seat to see
  Dora wash the doll.
"Bow-wow, bow-wow,"
  said Nip.
  "You will not wash me."

Jack, Mother, dog, tea, home, shop, toy," which later come into the early reading books.

In both word whole and sentence methods the names of the letters are learnt through a sensibly related writing-reading-programme.

Parallel with the first attempts at reading from cards or a book there is a certain amount of word matching, making sentences from sets of cardboard words, and sentence matching. This together with work-book exercises makes the approach to the printed sentences in the books a much easier matter. Where new words per page are controlled, and hence where repetition is adequate, it is possible for pupils to see printed on the blackboard the new words in the next page or pages they have to read. Moreover, they can, if necessary, write the new words before attempting the next page in the reading book. This may not be necessary for many pupils, but is a great aid to the less able readers. Finally, most teachers of the sentence method allow for some phonic training when a usable vocabulary has been mastered through the combined effect of meaning and visual impression.

## SUMMARY

The three methods of teaching reading are the phonic, the word whole (" look and say ") and the sentence methods.

The *Phonic Method* starts with letters and sounds which are used to form regular words and then sentences of a somewhat unreal, artificial form.

The *Whole Word Method* starts with meaningful words which are assimilated through pictures and actions and are soon used in sentences.

The *Sentence Method* is the complete opposite of the phonic method, for it starts with the large unit, the sentence, from which develops a study of the words of which it is composed, and finally, much later, a study of some of the letters or combinations of letters and sounds which make up the words.

The sentence method approach usually rests upon an organised, preliminary reading experience, such as a group study or centre of interest in which some of the common words occur.

Many teachers use a combination of methods such as phonic-word whole or sentence-word whole. The essential point is that children should not begin to learn reading by an analytic phonic method, but should begin with words or simple sentences.

## MODERN DEVELOPMENTS IN THE TEACHING OF READING

For the guidance of those concerned in the teaching of reading it will be beneficial to catalogue briefly the modern developments in reading instruction which are psychologically sound. These make the teaching of reading more effective and are characteristic of the best reading textbooks.

### (1) *The Use of Everyday Experiences as a Basis for Reading Material*

The psychological value of using the interests, the activities and the experiences of children, and information about children in other lands as progressive reading material has now been firmly established. What the child does and says, what he has himself seen and experienced through play, projects and stories, is so vitalised for him that when he meets these ideas embodied in the printed words he has an excellent chance of understanding what they mean. As has been shown in Chapters I and II, one of the most important factors in teaching children to read is to see that they are in possession of the ideas conveyed by phrases and sentences. We must ensure this by selecting from their experiences (where the environment is satisfactory) or by providing them with these experiences through talk and properly planned play. Unless this part of reading is satisfactorily accomplished, not a few children are bound to be confused and discouraged in their early introduction to printed words.

The use of experience or activity material, however, does not mean that the story element should be missing. My own opinion, substantiated by those of teachers, is that children like a mixture of both. They like to read about doing and making by other children, about their goings and comings in and out of home and school, about their pets ; but they also like some real stories with strong action. The interest created and the contextual value of a story are aids to reading—there are plenty of instances of pupils not recognising a word in an isolated form, but reading it at once when it is embedded with other words in an interesting story.

Nevertheless, a reading programme which gives pupils all stories and folk tales and omits entirely the experiential or activity material limits its possible success, particularly in the early stages of learning to read. Similarly, texts which keep too long to the everyday activity material and do not introduce stories soon enough are correspondingly impoverished. The correct scale of proportion appears to follow these steps :

(a) Keep to activities in the immediate experiences of the pupils when they begin reading, for the reality, simplicity and immediacy of their contacts aid recognition and understanding.

(b) Lengthen the printed material relating to the topics and introduce a story element.

(c) Extend the experiences to be dealt with beyond the home—to the shops, the streets, the zoo, the parks.

(d) Increase the amount of story content considerably.

(e) Include with stage (d) a certain amount of wider experience from other parts of the pupils' own country—visits to the seaside, to a port (to see ships, docks, etc.), to a farm, to an orchard, to a fishing village, to a mine, etc.

(f) Include information about children in other lands—main details of their lives and occupations through stories.

An example of this progression from a modern series of reading texts [1] as worked out in the various books is as follows :—

*Introductory Book.*—The main characters in the book are introduced by short sentences relating to such child activities as running, jumping, climbing, playing ball and hide-and-seek.

At this stage the very small amounts of reading matter are preceded and filled out by the teacher's story, before the actual reading matter is taken.

*Book I.*—The number of sentences per page is extended and the story element is increased. Games with pets—the cat, the kittens and the dog—are recounted, while more activities such as skipping, playing cricket, bathing the doll, visiting a shop to buy toys are described.

*Book II.*—In this book stories are longer and bring in other animals and pets like horses, rabbits, the hen and her chicks. More incidents in the children's lives are introduced and the range of experiences extends to the park, the pond, the zoo, the fields (flying kites).

*Book III.*—At this stage the reading matter, which covers a wider range of activities in the life of the pupils, includes topics like going to school, a visit to a railway station to see an engine, shopping, baking, preparing for a party, fun at the party, a visit to a fire station. Stories

---

[1] " Happy Venture Readers," a series of five books (Oliver and Boyd Ltd.).

occupy half of the book and are of the type, " The Tar Baby," "The Little Coal Truck."

*Book IV.*—In this book, although the everyday life of children still forms part of the reading material, the experiences have extended beyond the immediate vicinity of home and school. Thus the train journey, holidays at the seaside, visits to the circus, the merry-go-round, the day at the docks, all parallel the development of the interests of somewhat older children. Furthermore, the stories now tend to become longer, 15 or even 20 pages, with also a slight introduction to other lands, for example, Australia and India.

Modern reading texts endeavour to provide material relating to continuing centres of interest, and to maintain some continuity in the principal characters from book to book.

Finally, in the selection of material for the early reading books, there should be recognition of the ready response of children to rhythm, and ample opportunity should be provided for dramatisation. This last aspect is considerably facilitated if books contain a generous measure of direct speech.

## (2) *The Use of a Controlled Vocabulary*

*One of the most significant modern advances in the teaching of reading has been the use of a controlled vocabulary of common words in early reading books* and the consequent repetition of words used.

In the past some texts, particularly those exclusively using stories, have revealed a pronounced shortcoming in the matter of vocabulary control. For example, one series starts with 44 new words in the first book and then jumps to 218 new words in the next book. Because the vocabulary is so heavy and there are too many new words per page, many children are forced to proceed extremely slowly— some cannot proceed at all. Many of the less able ones need drilling repeatedly on the same page, and with the weakest pupils this results in memory reading. Even when the pupils have mastered a page with 12 or 16 new words upon it they are greatly discouraged to find that there are just as many new words they do not know upon the next page. Not only is training in adequate word recognition thereby neglected, but the pupils are discouraged by the difficulty of the task. *The only way to provide for progress for all pupils is by grading the reading material.*[1] If we agree to teach by the sentence method *it is essential that the vocabulary burden of the material in the early books should be adequately controlled.* The number of new words per page should be limited, and full provision should be made

*Analysis of Vocabulary Content of " Happy Venture Readers "*

|  | Approximate Number of Running Words. | Total Number of New Words. | Number of Pages in Book. |
|---|---|---|---|
| Introductory Book, *Fluff and Nip* | 602 | 43 | 20 |
| Book I, *Playtime* . . | 1,490 | 62 | 33 |
| Book II, *Our Friends* . | 2,744 | 96 | 50 |
| Book III, *Growing Up* . | 6,830 | 196 | 89 |
| Book IV, *Holiday Time* . | 12,740 | 339 | 121 |

for repetition of old words, so that maximum use can be made of learning through discrimination of visual patterns of words. Each page of reading material should, in the initial stages, present not more than 2 to 4 new words

[1] Grading of material in arithmetic, both as regards the numbers and the difficulties of the various phases of a process, is a firmly established principle, but we seem to be much slower in adopting a similar fundamental in the more important subject of reading.

embedded in known material. Later, as both stories and sentences lengthen, pupils can manage up to 5 or 6 new words on a page, provided the average throughout is not more than 3 to 4 new words per page. On page 57 for example, is an analysis of the vocabulary burden of a modern series of readers.

In the draft of the recent publication by the Scottish Council for Research in Education, namely, *Word Counts of Infant Readers*, the following was the analysis of the first two (or three) books of four different Infant Series.

| Reader A— | | | | Reader C— | | | |
|---|---|---|---|---|---|---|---|
| Introductory | . | . | 40 | Book I | . | . . | 214 |
| Book I | . | . . | 244 | Book Ia | . | . . | 244 |
| Book II | . | . . | 418 | Book II | . | . . | 564 |
| | | | 702 | | | | 1022 |

| Reader B— | | | | Reader D— | | | |
|---|---|---|---|---|---|---|---|
| Playway Books A and | | | | Book I | . | . . | 140 |
| B | . | . . | 95 | Book II | . | . . | 326 |
| Book I | . | . | 202 | | | | |
| Book II | . | . | 440 | | | | 466 |
| | | | 737 | | | | |

In the " Happy Venture Readers " the vocabulary content, *i.e.* of different words used in each book, runs as shown above, 43, 62, 96, 196, 339, in the five books respectively. This gradation gives every child a chance to make progress, and brighter children get on more quickly to new books. A too heavy vocabulary burden slows up children to the point of disappointment and confusion, with consequent loss of confidence and dislike of reading.

Psychological research shows that a most important factor in reading instruction is the initial attitude set up by the pupil. If success can be registered early, then the pupil will persist in further efforts. With a sentence method, success is best ensured by interesting material and by repetition of new words. A very light vocabulary burden in the early stages enables pupils to assimilate words as they appear and reappear on succeeding pages. For example, in the above series, the Introductory Book uses only 43 different words spread over 20 pages and making up a total of 602 running words, *i.e.* the repetitions of the 43 different words vary between 8 and 15 for each word.

The only reading material on the first page of this book is :

" Here is Dick " (picture).
" Here is Nip " (picture).

The words " here is " are repeated on that page and the pictures help the pupil to identify Dick and his dog, Nip. Then the next page introduces

" This is Dora."
" This is Fluff."

There is repetition of " is " and pictures aid in recognition of Dora and her cat Fluff.

On page 3 " Here is " again appears. " Nip " appears three times.

On page 4 " is " appears twice, " this " once, " Dick " three times, " Dora " once and " Nip " twice.

The new words are " run," " to " and " see."

In this way the pupil is given confidence in his recognition of words, while the adequate repetition allows gradual assimilation to take place without the soul-destroying drill on each page. A child thus reads a book relatively quickly, while bright children can read the first three books (20, 33 and 50 pages respectively) with such speed that great zest is added to the reading lesson—the idea of starting a new book is of paramount importance to young readers.

Completing one book quickly and passing to the next develops a sense of power and accomplishment.

In each book the new words that appear on each page as the book progresses are printed against the page number at the back of the book. For example, here is a section of the Word List (p. 41) of Book **I.**

| Page 2 | basket | Page 4 | stop |
|---|---|---|---|
| | for | | her |
| 3 | little | 5 | he |
| | kitten | | on |
| | Fluff's | | bad |

This is of inestimable value to the teacher who can take preparatory and revision work on the new words either from the blackboard or from the Word List itself.

The carrying on of the vocabulary from book to book is another essential feature of modern reading texts. For example, the 43 words in the Introductory Book of the above series are used in the next book, Book I, and similarly the 96 new words of Book II, as well as being adequately repeated in the book, are embedded throughout in the 105 words from the first two books. Thus natural, continued acquaintance with early material is maintained.

Careful grading of reading material not only ensures success for all pupils of varying intellectual calibres and verbal backgrounds, but it makes provision for group work for the different sections that inevitably occur in reading classes. The short books with their adequate control of the material are perfectly suited to groups of different reading levels within the one class.

## (3) *The Value of Illustrations*

There is not as yet sufficient realisation of the vital value of illustrations in the teaching of reading. Too often books contain insufficient pictures or are lacking in illustrations of real teaching and artistic worth. When learning to read the pupils obtain almost as much aid in recognising words from the right kind of illustration as they do from the various other cues. There should be but a small amount of print in early books, with plenty of bold, clear pictures specifically portraying the ideas of the printed material. Artists who really understand book illustrations for children, who are capable of painting pictures which interest children and who have the right concept of form, pattern and colour suited to the child's æsthetic-educational mind, are few in number.

Overleaf is a specimen of clear, bold illustration with a minimum of print.

### (4) *The Place and Use of Phonic Training in the Teaching of Reading*

As has been previously stated, there is now general agreement that phonic analysis of words by pupils should be postponed until they have (*a*) acquired a certain vocabulary through sight methods and (*b*) reached a certain *mental* age. When pupils have acquired a reading vocabulary of from 70 to 100 words they are able to read very simple material fairly fluently and they have formed an aptitude for the discrimination of the visual patterns of words. In addition they have formed the right attitude, namely reading by phrases or groups of words, so that understanding of what is read is developing—reading is not limited to saying words. At this stage some pupils may need the help of phonic training to further their reading ability.

Because of the recognised limitations of phonic analysis as an approach to reading (see pages 45 to 48), some teachers and educators have gone too far and have entirely discarded the use of phonics in the teaching of reading at any stage. This is psychologically unsound and indicates an extremist attitude based on ignorance—ignorance of the place and function of phonic analysis.

Here is Dick.

Here is Nip.

When a pupil assimilates a word into his reading vocabulary he should be able to

(*a*) recognise it by its visual pattern,
(*b*) pronounce it correctly,
(*c*) understand its meaning.

In a few cases pupils have reached (*a*) and (*b*) without (*c*); but this is not usual, as so much of the reading material in enlightened textbooks deals with common words within the speaking vocabulary of the pupils.

Now what is the exact function of phonic analysis in respect to these three capacities ? It can be best explained thus : if the pupil, on experiencing a new word in his reading (*i.e.* one of which he does not know the printed pattern), has previously heard the word and knows its meaning and pronunciation, then a phonic analysis of the word will bring it to his mind and he will be able to read it, particularly if the context is also helpful. But it should be noted that the aid provided by the phonic analysis is only supplementary to the cues of recognition of words through hearing and meaning. If, on the other hand, the word is an entirely unknown one (*i.e.* it is not known in respect to (*a*), (*b*) or (*c*) above), then it is doubtful, except with the brightest pupils, whether phonic analysis will help—the pupils may sound the word, but not get beyond that stage. This suggests three points :

(i) the limitations of phonic analysis,
(ii) the value of context in word recognition,
(iii) the value of verbal background in reading.

Without (ii) and (iii) phonic analysis cannot be very effective. Its chief value lies in enabling pupils to arrive at the correct pronunciation, which will bring into their mind " the total knowing " of the word as it appears in front of them in print. At this point in the teaching of reading many pupils are helped by this supplementary device of word recognition. Certain points, however, should be observed in the development of phonic analysis. With many children there is the need to produce a certain sensitivity to sounds in words before they can be expected to associate sounds with corresponding letters. This they do through extension of their meaning vocabulary, through hearing many words and through repeated reading of the words acquired in initial reading lessons. All children should be helped with the intriguing game, " I Spy ":

> " I spy with my little eye
> Something whose name begins with b " (sounding
> it phonetically).

Different letters can be exercised on different days. This, together with increased experience of words, will fit the pupil *at about mental age 6½ to 7 years* to be introduced to the connection between certain sounds and their printed symbols.

Slower and less intelligent pupils may need rhyming exercises and help through picture-word-sound association.

Another important point is that *phonics should always be used in close relationship to the material being read.* The study of lists of unrelated phonic words is to be deprecated. The best principle upon which to proceed is to associate the phonic work with the material the pupil is reading or likely to read in the near future. This practice does not aim at developing a hypothetical phonic ability, but at providing a help for pupils to recognise the words they are meeting day by day.[1]

Generally it is useful to approach phonic work in a play spirit. The teacher may ask pupils to look at the first letter of the word (*e.g.* t-all) and then at the remaining

[1] In the " Happy Venture Readers," lists of common phonic families are given at the end of the Second Book in the series, and these words provide a direct preparation for reading the material in that book and in the two succeeding books.

unit. Suggestions for other words may be taken from the children. Later an introduction to long vowels may be given.

In conclusion it should be remembered that phonic work should be given to the pupils only when it is required. It should be functional—that is, closely related to the actual reading material, and should not be taken before a vocabulary of sight words has been assimilated, a background of meaning developed and a sensitivity to letter sounds (in words themselves) created.

# CHAPTER IV

## ORGANISATION OF READING IN INFANT CLASSES

THE organisation for reading in the infant department or classes may be considered as catering for pupils between the ages of 5+ and 7+ years. It cannot be too strongly emphasised that there should not be any attempt to teach reading formally to children under the age of 5+, and even with most pupils of 5+ years the instruction should be largely of the incidental or preliminary kind. *All pupils under 5 years of age, irrespective of their intellectual brightness, should not be provided for in a formal scheme of reading.* Naturally, these under fives will take part in all kinds of games, see pictures, handle books, trace names, hear stories, talk about experiences and classroom doings, and engage in varied activities that will be an indirect preparation— and in the case of class projects and centres of interest a direct preparation — for actual reading lessons later on. The tendency to force bright children under 5, and to go beyond the experience and intellectual power of the duller pupils is, I believe, a real danger of the nursery class attached to an infant department, unless the headmistress is an understanding person with a knowledge of child psychology and a full realisation of the psychological requirements of the under fives. Many pupils would make greater progress in reading if there were no formal teaching in reading until 6 years of age.[1] Obviously, an aim such as this presupposes that the 5 to 6 period will embrace a very rich, extensive and varied preparatory reading programme.

[1] And as Miss Gardner shows, pupils taught by early informal method would gain in personality development and in later powers of persistence, intelligent application and understanding. See *Testing Results in the Infant School* by D. E. M. Gardner (Methuen).

Bearing in mind this basic principle of not forcing the young child beyond his intellectual and experiential level, we may pass to the *second* major aim, namely, that of making our organisation sufficiently flexible to provide for the varied range of intellectual abilities of our pupils and to cater for the varying rates of progress displayed by them. This involves knowing our pupils well, and it is here that for each pupil at the age of approximately 5½+ years the information obtained by means of the form in Chapter II, page 29, is so useful for grouping and organising within the classes in the initial stages of a reading scheme.

*Thirdly*, a carefully considered reading scheme embraces a mixture of individual and group methods, with perhaps more emphasis on group than on individual teaching. Although the individual consideration in matters of coaching and in material to be used must guide us at all stages of teaching reading, it is my experience, and with this many headmistresses and class-teachers agree, that children learning to read seem to make greater progress when in a group, even if the group is small, say only three or four children. Moreover, grouping does not preclude liberal individual help. The communal, "help each other" spirit, with mild competition and rivalry (providing the confidence of all members of the group is sustained), has a most stimulating effect upon powers of application and the desire to learn. Most young children learn almost as much from their colleagues as they do from their elders, if the environment is one of maximum opportunity.

As the mechanics of reading are mastered at different rates by different children there will be greater need to suit material to the individual reading ages.

*Fourthly*, the well-planned reading scheme with a combination of word whole and sentence methods in the initial period may be said to proceed by four stages.

*Stage I* may, according to the intellectual calibre and language background of the children in the school, follow, *from 5 to 5½ years of age*, either of two lines.

(*a*) With pupils who are not very bright and who come from rather poor homes, culturally, it is probably advisable to base the whole of the first stage (for the weakest ones up to 5¾ years) almost entirely on projects or centres of interest. No books will be used, but liberal numbers of pictures and posters, associated with the projects and with words and phrases to explain them, will be employed. Written notices about the incidents and activities connected with the developing project will help these children to become familiar with words as meaning something, and will lay the foundation indirectly for word recognition and word discrimination. The aim should be to associate spoken and written words in a natural and impelling, yet not too objective manner. Games involving words to extend the pupil's vocabulary, news sheets about the children's activities—" All About Us," " Our Weather Chart," " Our House "—will occupy the last three months of this stage.

(*b*) With pupils who are bright and who come from homes where the general language and cultural influences are good, the ground covered in Stage I will be somewhat greater and progress will be speedier. For example, children will learn with greater speed to recognise the names of their friends and the names of other children written on the blackboard. Names of animals and of children entering into stories and into the making of the toy house will be assimilated. Many of the bright children will be able to read such words as " Fluff, Nip, Dora, Dick, Tosh, and Mac," and simple sentences (printed as notices in appropriate positions) like

> This is Nip.
> This is Nip's house.
> The door is green.
> This is a window.
> The window is red.
> Nip is a dog.
> Fluff is a cat.

These brighter sections of pupils are usually ready to commence with a very simple reading book relatively quickly during this stage. Thus they may be started with such readers as *Fluff and Nip* (Introductory Book of " Happy Venture Readers "), *John and Mary* (" John and Mary Readers "), *Mac and Tosh*, Book I. Path to Reading.

While it is not advisable to hurry a child on to a book too soon—initial failure with books and a consequent dislike of reading must be avoided—many children like to feel that they can read from a book and they derive considerable stimulus from their first book. First books should be very simple and very short, and should contain a minimum of material with a maximum use of pictures. If possible, introductory books should be used containing material the words and phrases of which the children have to some extent experienced in their preliminary activities. The steps in dealing with the introductory book are as follows.

(i) The pupils learn, or have learnt, or revise the names of the characters in the book. For example, in the Introductory Book of the " Happy Venture Series," these names would be Dick, Nip, Dora, Fluff, Jane and Mother. A story is then told about the first page—this may be entitled " Dick and his dog Nip." The children are told about Dick and about Nip, about the way in which Nip plays with Dick, how he sits up and begs when he wants to play ball, etc., etc. A similar story can be told about Dora, her cat Fluff, and her doll Jane, and in subsequent pages further incidents dealing with these characters are recounted.

(ii) When the story about the first two pages has been told to the section of pupils commencing the book, the children gather round the teacher and the pictures are discussed. The teacher then reads the sentences several times until the children can associate the sentence with the picture, either the whole sentence or just certain words. *In these early stages the teacher should not aim at absolute accuracy*. Assimilation of words proceeds slowly, and teachers should not hurry or worry children if they do not know some of the same words on subsequent pages. Association with the words in slightly different contextual settings over a period of time brings a gradual and constant increase in reading vocabulary. There appears to be, with all young children, quite long periods of subconscious consolidation. Provided there is continuous consistent association with the words, and *mental effort on the part of the pupil*, progress will be made. From this it is obvious that the short frequent lessons are preferable to long ones and that the pupil's interest or power of application and concentration must be operating during the lessons. I emphasise this latter point, because there are some who would allow children simply to " float along," turning away or choosing some other activity when they meet difficulties. There is a midway course between the two extremes of *laissez-faire* and the driving, drilling, worrying methods of the " bad old " days. The child should be encouraged to go at his own pace, with time allowed for consolidation, but he must be trying, he must be putting forth mental effort.[1]

In the third aspect of this first stage a number of different groups of pupils will be similarly started with books, and they will be encouraged to read the few pages to the teacher and to one another under guidance.

*Stage II.*—This stage involves the entire class, which is now working in groups still with a combination of " look and say " and sentence methods. The weakest members of the more backward group, or groups, will require extra matching of word and phrase cards. Some groups may have started on the second book of a modern reading series in

[1] It is interesting to note that some of the intelligent children who fail in reading are those whose temperament or emotional attitudes interfere with their attempts to apply themselves with concentration and persistence to the job of discriminating and remembering word patterns. This is particularly so with pampered children whose initiative and independence have been undermined by having too much done for them. See *Backwardness in the Basic Subjects*, pp. 201-2.

which initial books are small in size and light in vocabulary
burden. Thus in the " Happy Venture Readers " the more
progressive groups of pupils will be working from Book I
(*Playtime*), that is, the second book in the Series, while other
groups will be using the Introductory Book (*Fluff and Nip*).
New words will be written on the blackboard as each group
deals with successive pages in different parts of either the
Introductory Book or Book I. Here the controlled vocabulary
reading books of the " Happy Venture Series " have a
distinct advantage over those which have not been compiled
on a scientifically selected and controlled vocabulary. A
teacher using an uncontrolled type of reader is unaware of
the new words on each page. As she takes pupils through
the successive pages of initial books it is somewhat of a " hit
and miss " affair, but with the *controlled vocabulary reader*
the number of new words per page is limited to two or
three, and the teacher can write these on the blackboard
or arrange for pupils to trace them from their writing pads.
Thus, in taking a group of pupils with page 15 of Introductory Book (*Fluff and Nip*) the teacher knows from the
Word List given at the end of the book (page 23) that the
only two *new* words on the page are " Jack " and " bring."
Or again, with a group of brighter pupils, who in this stage
are commencing to read pages 13 and 14 of Book I (*Playtime*), the new words listed in the Word List on page 41
are :—

> page 13, jump, jumps, do
> page 14, kittens, up

While it is the teacher's duty to try to anticipate word
difficulties and to prevent failure, elaborate word drills are
to be avoided. When the reading material is scientifically
constructed with proper attention to vocabulary burden,
word drills are not necessary—all that is required is brief
preliminary attention to the few new words appearing on
the pages about to be read. It is obvious that at this stage

pupils are beginning to reveal quite different rates of reading progress, and hence organisation should provide for this. Use books which suit particular groups, and allow pupils to change from group to group as their rate of progress indicates. Thus a pupil who is making rapid progress may be promoted quickly from a group still reading Introductory Book to one using Book I, or conversely a child who has not been able to maintain progress on Book I may be given a supplementary book of Introductory Book level—this obviates the disappointment of going back to a book already " read." Some individual work based on the reading material (suggestions for these are given in Appendix III) can be given to certain children. Matching, colouring, completing sentences, answering riddles, telling whether statements are true, etc., will all help to develop vocabulary and will afford useful preliminary training for silent reading. Workbook exercises prepared on sets of cards can easily be made by teachers along the lines suggested in Appendix III. Illustrations may be traced from this book and hectographed.

*Stage III.*—At this stage, that is when most pupils have reached the age of 6+, the work still proceeds in groups with appropriate individual work, but the range of reading ability is so great that each *group* will probably be working from a different book. Although sentence and " look and say " methods are largely used, yet this is the stage at which to introduce some phonic training.

Here two points stand out.

(*a*) All pupils should be given some phonic training. With brighter pupils the amount required will be small because of their larger vocabularies and their superior power of analysing and synthesising the sound elements of words. With these children phonic training will be largely incidental and will proceed rapidly.

(*b*) The phonics taught to all children should be functional phonics, that is, sound analysis of common words which they are reading, rather than some elaborate phonic scheme, designed to give children the key to successful reading—a quite erroneous conception of the purpose of phonics. Phonic practice should occupy only a few minutes of each lesson. As far as possible we should apply our phonic teaching to words which come within the meaning vocabulary of the pupils. Teachers should note how quickly pupils are able to deal with the phonic analysis and synthesis of familiar words—that is, familiar in meaning, but not in printed form. With such words many pupils need only the most cursory " breaking down " and " building up." The hearing of the familiar word, particularly if aided by contextual clue, helps the pupil to recognise it quickly when once he has analysed it into its constituent elements.

For example, I recall from recent work in an infant school how a pupil (age $6\frac{5}{12}$) reading a simple story was able to apply her phonic knowledge quickly to new (but familiar in meaning) words in this way.

> One day when Dick was in the gar-den—garden—, he saw a gr-e-at, greet—great light up in the sky.

This pupil, who was bright and had a good meaning vocabulary, was applying the functional phonic training which had been given at this stage. The words used by the teacher for phonic analysis had been taken from their reading books, and although only a certain amount of analysis and synthesis had been done, it enabled the pupil to tackle new words. Thus the " ea " in " great " had not been experienced, and the first attempt at synthesis was " greet " (as in seat which had been learnt). The use of intelligence, together with aid from the text, enabled the pupil to make the necessary modification.

Throughout this stage in the teaching of reading " the most practical phonic scheme is to base the study of phonic families on the words in the actual book being read and in the books to be read in the immediate future. Such phonic practice does not aim at developing a hypothetical phonic ability, but is a direct teaching of units to help pupils to recognise words they are meeting day by day." The golden rules in the teaching of phonics are :

(a) Do not commence phonic practice before pupils are intellectually ready for it—phonic analysis and synthesis require throughout the various steps increasing intellectual ability.

(b) Use phonic lists sparingly. Wherever possible link up or use phonic training in relation to continuous reading material. Breaking up and recombining words are only one aid in recognition— we should never neglect the major aid of the cue from continuous meaningful material, arranged in short sentences, and permeated by a story element.

In any phonic scheme the short vowel sounds will obviously be studied first. With bright children most of these groups of words will be taken in their stride. What is most important to all children is to be shown how to attempt an analysis and synthesis of words ; thus acquaintance with the structure of " r-un " and " s-ing " will help the pupil to try " r-un-ning " when he experiences it in his reading material. The introduction to common sound units is of immense value to many pupils; thus the " -ar " in c-ar is the same " -ar " in " st-ar-t," and if pupils have been introduced to " st " as in " stop," " st-ill," " st-and," then it is a very easy step to quickly analyse and recombine (almost automatically) the elements of " start." As the child proceeds with his reading, much of the phonic analysis and synthesis will be done almost unconsciously, and will provide correct, indirect aid in the process of reading. The main thing in phonic teaching is *not* to allow phonic analysis, with its sounding of words to become anything more than an aid to reading. *It must receive only its correct proportion of attention, yet it is an aid with which nearly all children should be provided.*

The progression of phonic practice might profitably follow, at this stage of reading, that laid down in Book I (second book in the series) of the " Happy Venture Readers." Pupils would thus be introduced by a series of steps to graded word families in this way :

*Groups of words with these endings*

| | | | |
|---|---|---|---|
| c-*at* | s-*it* | g-*ot* | d-*og* |
| b-*ig* | c-*an* | l-*ip* | h-*op* |
| m-*ud* | c-*ap* | b-*ed* | w-*et* |
| l-*eg* | c-*up* | b-*ag* | d-*id* |
| p-*in* | m-*en* | d-*ug* | |
| s-*and* | f-*ell* | w-*ill* | m-*ust* |
| n-*est* | s-*ing* | s-*ick* | b-*ack* |
| n-*eck* | d-*uck* | b-*all* | f-*ull* |

With most of the brighter groups of pupils there need be little actual phonic practice with these groups, but weaker readers may require to go more slowly over these steps and to be introduced to as many common words as possible with these endings. Brighter pupils are always able to make more effective transfer of knowledge than duller ones.

The phonic practice, *which occupies only a few minutes of each lesson,* may take the form of rhymes constructed by the teacher from the group of words under consideration. *E.g.* -ot group (in the 1st step) —

Spot, Spot,
fell in the pot
and got hot.

I can say :
" Rain, rain, go away
And come on Mother's washing day."

Pupils may be encouraged to give lines or groups of

words which rhyme. As the phonic steps progress, so use may be made of well-known nursery rhymes and songs.[1]

At first simple rhymes :

> Pat-a-cake, Pat-a-cake, baker's *man*,
> *Bake* me a *cake* as fast as you *can* ;
> Prick it and pat it and mark it with T,
> And put it in the oven for Tommy and me.

Later longer rhymes such as :

> Wee Willie Winkie
>> Runs through the *town*,
> Upstairs and *down*stairs
>> In his night *gown*.
> Rapping at the window,
>> Crying through the *lock*,
> " All the children in their beds
>> Past eight o'*clock*."

In later steps pupils are introduced to common consonant combinations, *e.g.* ch, ck, sh, st, th and long vowels, *e.g.* came, make, white, ride, line, may be given.

The bulk of the phonic teaching at this stage will be given to groups, and distributed according to the progress being made by the pupils. A little class teaching of certain phonic families may be helpful.

Additional use will be made at this stage of prepared reading cards, which are a natural way of linking reading, English and writing. These cards not only provide facility for extending the vocabularies of the pupils, but they give practice through writing of some words with which pupils might not be quite familiar in their reading.

*Stage IV.*—At this stage all pupils should be able to **read** a simple book with a certain amount of fluency and

---

[1] The teacher will find *Nursery Rhymes* (Oliver and Boyd Ltd) and *Mother Goose's Book of Nursery Rhymes and Songs* (Dent) useful sources.

comprehension, so that individual reading books from various series can be introduced.

Parallel with this development there will be the need to acquaint pupils with other consonant combinations such as -nk, -ng, -ar and with common consonant and vowel digraphs such as wh and ee.

Here, too, familiarity with phonic families may come through nursery rhymes or through puzzles. All practice will be short and incidental, never detracting from the main objective of encouraging and allowing pupils to read continuous material from appropriate books.

## SUPPLEMENTARY READING MATERIAL

Considerable use may now be made of graded supplementary reading books to give further practice for children who have progressed well with the class textbooks in use. A stimulus to the reading of simple supplementary books is to allow pupils to keep a record on prepared cards of the books read. As at this stage reading comprehension should be developed and tested, it is useful to have very simple exercises based on the supplementary texts in order to direct the reading and, at the same time, to check the results of the reading, much of which will be done in groups to other pupils. With more advanced children a considerable amount of reading will be done silently, and here again it is advisable to motivate it and to provide ingenious methods of testing.[1]

[1] See *Backwardness in the Basic Subjects*, pp. 248 to 276, for suggested ways of motivating and testing silent reading. A useful summary of reading devices is to be found in *Reading Aids through the Grades*, Bureau of Publications, Teachers College, Columbia University, New York City. See pp. 38 to 39 and pp. 43 to 50 for exercises designed to aid and test comprehension.

# CHAPTER V

# ORGANISATION OF READING IN
## JUNIOR CLASSES

IN junior classes of pupils 7+ to 11+ years the important objective, particularly with the first and second classes of pupils aged 7+ to 9+, is to ensure continuity of reading instruction from the Infant Department. The bulk of the pupils promoted from infant classes or departments will have mastered the mechanics of reading, and if suitable graded reading material is available they will continue to make progress. But there will always be from all infant classes a percentage of children, from 15 per cent. to as high as 40 per cent. in some areas, who are still having difficulty with the mechanics of reading. Occasionally this percentage of backward readers is due to bad teaching, sometimes to environmental conditions, such as absence or continuous change of school, but most often, as I have shown elsewhere,[1] it arises from the fact that these children have not matured at the same rates as their companions either in general intelligence or in the special abilities required in learning to read. It is therefore vital that these groups of children, backward in reading and spelling, should continue to receive instruction similar in kind and in quantity to that of which their friends were able to take full advantage in the infant classes. Unless these children secure this careful attention they either stagnate in verbal attainments or, in some cases, lose the little ground previously gained in their infant groups. Furthermore, unless they

[1] *Backwardness in the Basic Subjects* (Oliver and Boyd Ltd., 1942) in Chapter IX. Causes and symptoms of disability in reading are considered in detail, and in particular the differing rates of maturation in special abilities in learning to read are explained, and illustrative cases of backward readers are described.

progress in reading, it is likely that their personality development and the whole of their instruction in junior classes or junior departments will be marred by their backwardness in reading. Thus organisation of reading in the lower levels of the junior school is a matter of paramount importance—in fact more important than any other subject or activity. It is only by attention to the right methods and materials for these backward readers that we can prevent personality deterioration, which in some cases results in a compensating outlet of delinquency. Furthermore, the right treatment, early, prevents backwardness in reading becoming a barrier to progress in written composition, spelling and even arithmetic, and it obviates later illiteracy in the senior school, and with some, illiteracy in adult life.

## ORGANISATION

The problem of catering effectively for all grades of reading attainments amongst pupils of 7+ to 9+ is almost as much a responsibility of the administrator and the training college lecturer as it is one for the school staff. For in the first instance there should be more flexibility allowed between infant and junior classes or departments—the hard and fast age of transfer should not prevail in the cases of a small number of children who, if left for six or nine months longer with infant teachers using infant methods, would profit immensely in their reading instruction. Furthermore, there should be, in lower junior classes, teachers who are not only sympathetic towards modern infant school methods, but who are well informed about methods and materials for teaching reading at infant school levels, and who have had some experience with pupils of 6+ to 7+.[1]

[1] In this respect it is encouraging to see that some training colleges have taken up this problem and now train a body of students capable of teaching over a pupil age range of 5+ to 9+. These students take a course in child psychology, and one dealing with teaching methods and materials applicable to pupils aged 5 to 9. They do some teaching practice in both infant classes and lower junior classes.

Finally, for that small core of backward readers who present more than usual difficulty even up to the age of 10+ years, education committees should provide opportunities for selected teachers to attend a full course (of eight or ten weeks) in diagnostic testing and in remedial teaching methods. Even one such qualified teacher in a junior school could be of inestimable value in diagnosing the difficulties of very backward readers, in planning remedial teaching for them, and in giving general guidance to his or her colleagues upon remedial methods and materials.

## PLANNING BY CLASS TEACHERS

There are signs that improved organisation is very slowly coming into being in some of the more progressive areas, but even when this is universal to the education system, it will still be necessary for the class teacher in the junior school to plan scientifically his reading instruction. Briefly, the steps in this planned reading programme are : (1) Use of a graded reading test; (2) planning of methods and division of groups on the basis of the reading test results ; (3) selection of appropriate materials ; (4) maximum practice in oral and silent reading for particular groups ; (5) testing the progress of selected children.

## USE OF GRADED WORD-READING TEST

The first step in this scientific planning, the intelligent use of a graded reading test, is probably only necessary, as a universal measure, for pupils in the first and second classes in junior departments. Inevitably there will always be in classes of pupils of 7+ to 9+ a wide range in reading attainments. Perhaps the one exception to this will be in a large junior school, where the enrolment permits of three streams and where the first year A and second year A classes are sufficiently homogenous to contain pupils all of whom have no difficulty with the mechanics of reading; but even in such classes it is my experience that there still exists a fairly wide range in speed and accuracy in silent reading.

In most classes in the lower part of the junior school the range of reading attainments is usually about 4 years, and not infrequently 5 or even 6 years; that is to say, there are some pupils aged 7, 8 or 9 who have not progressed beyond a 5+ reading level, while there are others who can read almost as well as the average 10-, 11- or 12-year-old pupil. Indeed, if we test an entire age group in the junior school, we invariably find a larger spread in reading ages than this. Recently I tested 59 boys *between the ages of* 10 *and* 11, and their reading ages ranged from the cases of two boys who had only reached reading levels of 5·1 and 5·2 years respectively to a group of 6 boys whose power of word recognition in reading was 13·1, 13·1, 13·2, 13·4, 13·5, 13·5 years—a range of from poorest to best in the entire group of 8·4 years. The detailed distribution of results was as follows :—

| Reading Ages. | Number of Pupils. |
|---|---|
| 5-6 | 2 |
| 6-7 | 2 |
| 7-8 | 4 |
| 8-9 | 4 |
| 9-10 | 4 |
| 10-11 | 7 |
| 11-12 | 17 |
| 12-13 | 13 |
| 13-14 | 6 |

As might be expected, these 10-year-old boys were spread throughout four different classes.

Now, it is a simple matter to find out the exact reading age of each pupil in one's class—information which is invaluable in planning methods, selecting material and checking the progress of the weaker pupils. In Appendix I (pages 92 and 93) is set out in print, varying in size to suit the ages of the testees, a graded reading vocabulary test. The words in this test were selected, after careful preliminary trials and testing with groups of pupils between the ages of 6 and 14+ years, from a much larger body of words. The test thus represents a scientifically selected sample of words, of increasing difficulty, that will give an accurate estimate of a pupil's power of word recognition, which obviously is the very basis of his ability to read and understand any printed material. The test words increase by a known amount of difficulty from one word to the next within each group, and from one group to another. This even increase in difficulty was obtained from the calculation of the percentages of passes made for each word by the pupils in each age group from 6 to 13 years.

From this data it was possible to allot ten words, gradually increasing in difficulty, to each age group from 5 to 6 years up to 13 to 14 years.

It is thus apparent that the words which constitute the test provide the teacher with a measuring instrument of carefully selected, scientifically graded units, by use of which he can determine the exact level a pupil has reached in his power of word recognition. As the detailed instructions show on pages 94 to 99, we aim at discovering the total number of these words that the testee can read. We then calculate his reading age on that basis. So that *reading age for word recognition* is obtained in this way :—

$$\frac{\text{the number of words } \textit{correctly} \text{ read}}{10} + 5 \text{ years.}$$

There are 10 words in each age group from 5 years onwards, and 5 years are added to the score for the pretesting years. The testing usually takes about five or six minutes per testee, so that at the end of three reading lessons (thirty-five or forty minutes each) the teacher will have a complete list of reading ages of the entire class.

The criticism that the words not being in a continuous meaningful form (*i.e.* sentences or paragraphs) are therefore not in a setting familiar to the testees is not a valid one. The form of the test does not disturb testees, and experiments show that even if all words were couched in sentences the actual reading ages obtained would not materially alter. In all probability the high degree of accuracy revealed by the test, not only of relative accuracy from pupil to pupil, but of reliability, might show a slight decline if the sentence form of testing were used.

Extensive use of graded reading vocabulary tests shows that this type of test is a most accurate way of estimating the level reached by pupils in the mechanics of reading. Hence teachers are able to use the results from the test for three things—as a basis upon which to divide their classes into sections and groups for reading, as a guide in the selection of reading books, and as a check upon the progress made by backward readers over a given period.

## METHODS AND MATERIALS

It is apparent from the range of reading ages which we obtain from testing pupils in lower junior classes that reading cannot be taken simply as a class lesson. It is essential that the reading lessons should be planned to give maximum practice with materials suited to the pupils' reading ages. Some will require much oral practice with very simple reading books, while others will be sufficiently advanced to be able to do a considerable amount of motivated silent reading. The most effective organisation

[1] For a detailed consideration of the use of the Graded Word Reading Test and the relation of test results to the use of the graded series *Wide Range Readers*, see " Reading in the Junior School ", F. J. Schonell, *Educational Review*, Feb. 1950.

for this is a combination of class sections for reading and group reading. The pupils should be divided into two or three sections on the basis of their reading ages, and appropriate textbooks used for each section.[1] With these reading books suited to the range of reading ability in each section it will be possible for the teacher to do a certain amount of oral reading instruction for the benefit of pupils in each group, while other sections are engaged in individual card work or in silent reading checked by questions and exercises. To obtain still more intensive practice for the weaker members, the class may be divided into even smaller reading units, namely, five or six reading groups. Each group should contain pupils of approximately similar reading ages, and in this way we can still further suit the material to the reading level of the pupils and arrange for more practice for the backward readers. In group reading it is possible to make use of the short supplementary texts which firms publish at a relatively low cost. These simple, short, graded stories, each constituting a book, are enjoyed by the pupils who have a sense of achievement as they complete book after book.

In the junior school both class reading texts and

[1] For junior school pupils who are backward readers and whose reading ages come within the range $5\frac{1}{2}$ years to $7+$ years, the word-controlled series of *Happy Venture Readers* is most effective in so far as each book is specially compiled to provide for a gradual growth in reading age. With the most backward of these children it may be necessary to use, firstly, graded card material to aid word recognition through word, phrase and sentence matching, and, secondly, simple exercises to encourage, from the outset, the development of comprehension of what is read. For groups of pupils whose reading ages range from 7 to 12 years teachers will find a new series of books—*The Wide Range Readers*, by F. J. Schonell and P. Flowerdew (Oliver and Boyd), most helpful. The *Wide Range Readers* consist of two parallel series (Green Books and Blue Books) of books specially prepared with vocabulary control to provide for the spread of reading in junior schools. Book I for reading age 7 to $7\frac{1}{2}$; Book II, $7\frac{1}{2}$ to 8; Book III, 8 to $8\frac{1}{2}$; Book IV, $8\frac{1}{2}$ to 9; Book V, 9 to 10; Book VI, $10+$ to $11+$.

supplementary reading material should only be purchased in groups of ten or twelve books. It is much better to have a large number of smaller sets of reading books covering wide ranges of reading ability than to have limited numbers of sets of forty-five or fifty copies of the same books.

The actual technique employed in section reading and in group reading in junior classes, with suggestions for remedial material to suit reading ages from 5 to 9 years, is given in detail in *Backwardness in the Basic Subjects*, pp. 237-244.

## CHECKING PROGRESS

Our major aim in the junior school should be to see that all pupils progress in reading. Unless we make this our first objective it is possible for some children to remain in their classes in junior departments month after month and to make little or no progress in this all-important subject. Unless our organisation is such as to permit maximum practice for all pupils with suitable material, then some pupils will " stagnate verbally," and will pass through the 7+ to 10+ period and be transferred to senior classes or senior schools as non-readers. In spite of all efforts we make to use the most effective methods, to arrange for individual help and practice, and to provide appropriate reading materials, we are occasionally faced at the end of the junior school stage with a small residue of non-readers who, through a combination of circumstances, are as yet illiterates. But this small residue should not be more than 2 per cent.— it certainly should not be 8 or even 10 per cent., which is the figure one not infrequently finds in some areas. It is obvious that a senior school receiving in the mass 10 per cent. of non-readers and a further 5 or 6 per cent. of weaker readers from its contributory junior schools is handicapped from the outset in its objectives of giving suitable post-primary education. It should therefore be the aim of each junior school to check *the progress of its weak readers every six months* in order to see that reading retardation is being reduced to the lowest possible margin.

The graded reading vocabulary test, already used for grading, may be used here. There is no likelihood of practice effects vitiating the results of the test, for each word represents a sample of reading material at a particular level of difficulty. As the pupil makes progress so he is able to read an increasing number of words. If the pupil is not making progress in reading, then it does not matter how often he is given the test—his result remains approximately the same.[1] Thus the test may be used to check the progress of the ten or twelve or even twenty weakest readers in the school. With proper organisation of reading lessons and provision of suitable reading books it will be found that in six months some of the pupils will have made remarkable progress ; it is not uncommon to find pupils increase their reading age by as much as eighteen or twenty months in six calendar months. Others will have made average progress, *i.e.* a gain commensurate with the increase in chronological age, while a few will not have made more than a very slight increase, *e.g.* from reading age 6·1 to 6·2 or from reading age 6·11 to 7·2. The lack of progress of this last-named group is a challenge to the teacher—obviously these pupils need some additional stimulus ; perhaps a new attack on the subject, with parental co-operation, is required. Perhaps more individual help and additional periods of reading practice are necessary, in which case reading practice during other lessons, the help of older boys or girls, with an extra few minutes here and there from the teacher, might produce the desired improvement. With all such pupils we should look closely at the method we are using—possibly more writing and tracing are required, or it may be that

[1] Naturally in giving the test, either initially or at a later retesting, the teacher should not read to the pupil nor teach him the words which he does not know. Retests of groups of children with the graded word test showed a high reliability ratio, namely, ·96.

further systematic phonic work would help others. With this very backward group some attempt at a more detailed diagnosis of their condition should be made before continuous failure hardens into frustration and creates emotional barriers which are difficult to dissipate. It is suggested that teachers should read Chapters VII to X in *Backwardness in the Basic Subjects* for an understanding of the lines upon which diagnosis and modification of teaching methods might profitably proceed.

Finally, we should not overlook the far-reaching effect of extending the pupil's speaking and meaning vocabulary in general. The wider we can make his verbal background the better is his chance to progress in reading. The keen class teacher might of course retest her whole class after an interval of nine or twelve months. It is satisfying to see how much progress some pupils have made, while at the same time with other pupils it is a further stimulus to teaching powers and to our skill in adaptation when an objective assessment reveals how little they have profited from instruction.

We should always keep in mind the fact that reading is only a means to an end. Pupils learn to read, at first largely orally and later silently, in order to understand the printed word. The ultimate objective is to understand the ideas, to appreciate the story, or to follow instructions, or to enjoy the beauty of the words or the rhythm, or to gain information from the written words of the author. Thus, as soon as a child has mastered the mechanics of reading, he should be introduced to directed silent reading, increasing in amount as his actual technical skill in reading increases. All kinds of stimuli and motives can be introduced to direct and vitalise the silent reading. These motives are manifold, and vary from the absorbing interest of a story to the sheer delight of understanding the clues in a treasure hunt. It is the teacher's job to make reading as real, meaningful and purposeful as possible. Occasionally, as the pupils progress through the school, it is necessary to check their powers of silent reading. Are they able to understand and use what they are reading ? In this respect the sparing and occasional use of a silent reading test [1] may reveal definite difficulties and weakness on the part of some children who may have mastered the mechanics of reading, but who are not yet able to use their newly acquired tool with the fullest effect. The pupils need some help in learning to read silently for a variety of purposes.

## FINAL OBJECTIVES

As our final objective we should remember that the curriculum in the junior school should provide activities and experiences that will cater for personal needs and stimulate a social awareness. To achieve this the reading programme must be at the same time planned yet flexible, directed yet varied—our aim should be to provide all children with as many experiences as possible. The enrichment of language background through oral work connected with activities will be the surest way of aiding our reading programme. For this reason we cannot dissociate the planning of reading from the various centres of interest or environmental studies based on the requirements of the children. Group studies of such topics as " Our clothes," " The story of books," " The story of time," " How we travel," " How people live," " The market," " The post office," " Wheat and bread," " The farmer," " Shops," " The games of boys and girls," " Our town," can give rise to an immense amount of selected, informative reading for pupils of different ages. Moreover, the knowledge thus gained and the attitudes

[1] Suitable silent reading tests which cover a variety of aspects of silent reading—for detail, for general impression, for inference, for following instructions—available in booklets which can be used and reused for different classes, are obtainable from Oliver and Boyd Ltd. : *Silent Reading*, Test A (for ages 7 to 11) ; *Silent Reading*, Test B (for ages 9 to 14).

thus formed should be of great value to pupils later if we can evolve an enlightened, sensible, realistic curriculum for out post-primary schools.[1]

Teachers will find that *Projects for the Junior School*, Books 1 to 4 (R. K. and M. I. R. Polkinghorne) contain helpful reading matter for use in conjunction with group studies.

In catering for the personal reading needs of pupils it is essential that teachers should guide boys and girls in their choice of reading material. Many a child has been turned away from a particular book for ever because he has started it too early, and many a child has failed to develop a stable and steadily improving reading habit because of lack of help in selecting books appropriate to his reading ability and his stage of mental growth.[2]

Not only do pupils need guidance in what will suit their attainments and interests at particular ages, but they also need to be weaned gradually from the " 3d. blood " and " Peg's paper " stage ; they need to be adroitly introduced to Henty, Ballantyne, Marryat, Stevenson, etc., so that eventually not a few of them will realise that these writers provide the same kinds of thrills and adventures, but that they add something—perhaps extra vividness of characterisation, perhaps interesting historical and geographical knowledge. I believe that psychologically the " 3d. blood " stage is normal and necessary and that pupils should be allowed to read such material if they desire, but, without being either priggish or unpsychological in our knowledge of boys and girls, our aim should be to lead them to read good literature.

In giving reading guidance much more could be done by teachers in the grading of books in school libraries and in introducing pupils to suitable groups of books by the

[1] See *The Social Approach to the Curriculum*, by C. Fletcher (The English New Education Fellowship).

[2] Here guidance can be obtained from *What Boys and Girls like to Read*, by A. J. Jenkinson (Methuen).

use of simple direction cards. This same lack of systematic aid to young readers is noticeable in some of the juvenile sections of public libraries—the book for the eight-year-old is found alongside the book for the fifteen-year-old.

Finally, the reading programme must satisfy the growing intellectual curiosity of the older pupils. Hence in addition to good fiction there must be books of social, general, scientific, historical and geographical interest, such as these :

*Natural History.—Let's Watch the Birds* (Univ. London Press), *Beaver People* (U.L.P.), *The Romany Books* (U.L.P.), *Stories of the Wild* (McDougall Educ. Co.), *The Wonderland of Nature* (Grant Educ. Co.), *Fabre's Book of Insects* (Tudor Pub. Co., New York), *Wild Life Ways* (U.L.P.), *The Observer's Book of British Butterflies* (Warne & Co.), *Cranes Flying South* (Puffin Book), *The Adventures of Sajo and her Beaver People* (Grey Owl (Peter Davies)), *Red Ruff* (Puffin Book), *Starlight* (Puffin Book), *Panther* (Collins).

*Everyday Science.—Lively Things for Lively Youngsters* (Cassell), *Science in the Home* (Oliver and Boyd), *Modern Marvels Encyclopedia* (Collins), *The Science of Life* (Collins), *Iron and Steel* (Dent), *The Microbe Man* (Life of Pasteur (Heinemann)), *The Insect Man* (Life of Fabre (Heinemann)), *The Radium Woman* (Life of Madame Curie (Heinemann)).

*General Knowledge.—The Wonder World Encyclopedia* (Collins), *Newnes' Pictorial Knowledge, Children's Encyclopedia, Reading to Learn* (The Macmillan Co.), *A Book of Interests* (Nisbet), *Palisay the Potter and other Stories* (Oxford Univ. Press), *The Story of Gold* (O.U.P.), *Houses* (Dent), *The Story Book of Wheels* (Dent).

*Historical.—He went with Marco Polo, He went with Christopher Columbus* (Harrap), *Black on White* and *What Time is it?* (a history of printing and clocks respectively, translated from the Russian ; pub. Routledge). *A History of Everyday Things*, 4 vols. (Batsford), *How Man became a Giant* (Routledge), *Everyday Life in the New Stone, Bronze and Early Iron Ages* (Batsford), *Columbus Sails* (Puffin

Story Book), *The Children's Heroes* (" *Bonnie Prince Charlie*," " *Baden Powell* " (Nelson & Co.)), *No Other White Man* (Puffin Story Book).

*Geographical.—Exploring New Fields* (The Macmillan Co.), *The U.S.S.R.* (Univ. London Press), *Young Fu of the Upper Yangtze* (Hutchinson), *The Splendid Journey* (Heinemann), *Tents in the Wilderness* (Harrap), *Men of the Icebreaker Sedov* (Hutchinson), *Coconut Island* (Puffin Story Book), *Greentree Downs* (Puffin Story Book), *David Goes to Zululand* (Puffin Story Book), *Stormalong* (Puffin Story Book), *North After Seals* (Puffin Story Book), and stories of this kind.

Not only should there be a well-stocked class library but pupils from the age of 9 + should be encouraged to use the public library. Some progressive towns have arranged shelves of books suitable for children of different ages. The library committees realise that their juvenile reading members are as important as their adult members and cater for them in an effective and attractive way.

The well-read child who can use his reading ability to the fullest extent, both for gaining information and for his own leisure pursuits, is likely to make an effective adult member of a democratic community.

---

## APPENDIX I

# GRADED READING VOCABULARY TEST

Pages 92-93

| | | | | |
|---|---|---|---|---|
| tree | little | milk | egg | book |
| school | sit | frog | playing | bun |
| flower | road | clock | train | light |
| picture | think | summer | people | something |
| dream | downstairs | biscuit | shepherd | thirsty |
| crowd | sandwich | beginning | postage | island |
| saucer | angel | ceiling | appeared | gnome |
| canary | attractive | imagine | nephew | gradually |
| smoulder | applaud | disposal | nourished | diseased |
| university | orchestra | knowledge | audience | situated |

physics    campaign    choir    intercede    fascinate

forfeit    siege    recent    plausible    prophecy

✗ colonel    soloist    systematic    slovenly    classification

genuine    institution    ×pivot    conscience ×heroic

pneumonia    preliminary    antique    ✗ susceptible ∠ enigma

oblivion    scintillate    ✗ satirical    sabre    beguile

↗ terrestrial    ↗ belligerent    adamant    sepulchre ⩔ statistics

miscellaneous ×procrastinate    tyrannical    evangelical    grotesque

ineradicable    judicature    preferential    ≠ homonym    fictitious

rescind    metamorphosis    somnambulist ∥ bibliography∥ idiosyncrasy

100%/₁₁

⁹⁰/₁₀⁵*

# INSTRUCTIONS FOR GIVING THE GRADED READING VOCABULARY TEST

## PRECAUTIONS

THE test should be given to one testee at a time and the testing should take place in an atmosphere of quiet and calm. Distraction prevents the testee from concentrating upon the material and it may prevent the tester from hearing accurately the pupil's pronunciation of the more difficult words. Only the printed form of the test, as given on pages 92 and 93 should be used, as in this form care has been taken to select a size of print appropriate to progressive reading levels.

## PRELIMINARY ATTITUDE

The most important point to observe in giving the test is that an atmosphere of friendliness and co-operation should prevail between tester and testee. This, in most cases, is easily and quickly achieved by a smile, a few friendly words, a greeting, a jest—any such suitable attitude to reassure the child that this is a joint affair between you and him, that it is in no way a vital examination, and that you will be pleased if he will just try to read as many words as he can. I always call the pupil by his Christian name—it is more personal and is one way of establishing rapport.

After taking the child's name and age, frame an introduction on these lines : " Well, Jim, I've a lot of words here and I want to see how many you can read. The first words are fairly easy and then they get a little harder. Now, let me see how many you can read, please. Read across the page." (Quickly run your finger from word to word across the *first* five words with which the testee is to commence.)

Obviously there must be some minor modification of the initial approaches to suit individual cases. If one can see (or has had previous knowledge) that the testee is nervous and apprehensive, it is usually advisable to talk to the pupil for a little while, asking her a few questions about herself. " Do you live far from the school, Bessie ? " " Have you got any brothers and sisters ? " " You're lucky having two brothers, I've only got one," (or some such remark appropriate to the case). Obviously, too, with backward readers or with very dull children, one would omit the opening remarks about the first words being easy. It is also necessary with such pupils to praise liberally. " Good, that's right, now try the next line." A halting reader, who is apprehensive of his own achievements or of what you are thinking, may also need additional sympathetic encouragement.

The examiner must use his knowledge of child psychology to detect quite early the child's attitude towards him and the test, and to mould his opening statements in accordance with the demands of the situation.

## RECORDING

Young testees up to the age of 9 should start the test from the beginning—the printed form should be squarely placed in front of the child—and the examiner should record the responses on a separate sheet. The recording should not be made too obvious; it should not be so apparent that it might distract the pupil. At the same time the recording should be carefully and systematically done for each pupil. *Do not try to count orally the number of words correctly (or incorrectly) read by the testee, and do not try to score on odd bits of paper.* The record should be so made that the calculation of the number of words correctly read, and hence of the reading age, may be done at some convenient break or pause after the conclusion of the testing. The most convenient way of recording is to make a dot for each word correctly read and a cross for each word wrongly read. The marks should be made in rows of five following the pattern of the test—a small space left after each ten words will later facilitate finding the total words correctly read.

*E.g.* Peter S., $8\frac{5}{12}$.

```
 .     .     .     .     .
 .     .     .     .     .

 .     .     .     .     .
 .     .     .     .     .

 .     .     .     x     x
 .     .     .     x     x

 .     x     x     x     x
 x     x     x     x     x
```

Total score, 29 words.

## GIVING THE TEST

If the pupil reads too fast for the purpose of recording, he may be asked to read more slowly, or to reread a line some words of which the examiner was not sure about. There should not be any prompting of the pupil during his reading of the words. Allow the pupil adequate time if he wishes to analyse and recombine the words. Some pupils are very slow readers, but show a fairly well-developed power of word analysis and synthesis if given sufficient time—this is one of the things revealed by the test. The pupil should not be hurried, and self-corrections should be counted as correct. *At the same time any attempt at coaching or teaching a testee should be studiously avoided.* Thus a slow pupil reading the word " shepherd " may say " she (as in she) p-her-d," then half say to himself " she(e)pherd," finally giving the correct form " shepherd "; this is counted as correct.

On the other hand a pupil reading the word " postage "

may say " post (as box) age " instead of " post (as in low)
age," and the examiner, not quite sure of the testee's pronunciation, may ask him to say it again. If the pupil
repeats the first-named form the word is counted as wrong.
Asking for a repetition of the word should be used only
when the examiner is not sure of what the pupil has
said. If the word is clearly said wrongly, as " can'ary "
instead of " ca'nary," then there is no need to ask for a
repetition. Asking the pupil to reread the word or words
should not be used to indicate " You had better look
at it again, there is something wrong with it." The
only cases in which one would allow this is when an
obviously bright pupil or good reader makes a slip in an
earlier word. For example, a bright 10-year-old pupil
reading quickly may leave the " s " off " downstairs,"
but on being asked again to read the word will usually
give it correctly.

Words should not be pronounced for pupils even when
they stumble over them. The rare occasion on which a
word should be pronounced for a pupil is in the early
stages of testing with a hesitant pupil, who is apprehensive
and lacking in confidence. One may then pronounce a
word with the object of encouraging him to move on to
other words with which he may be able to register a success,
and thus give him confidence to try further words. Usually
however the injunction, " We will leave that one and try this
word," is sufficient.

The usual pronunciation of words (e.g. see the Oxford
Dictionary) is accepted. Guessing should not be discouraged ; in fact, intelligent guessing is one means by
which pupils make progress in reading. Pupils above the
age of 9 years may be allowed to commence the test at the
third, fourth or fifth group of ten words (according to
age), i.e. a 10-year-old may commence at " saucer," a
13-year-old may commence at " physics." The point at
which the testee should commence is left to the discretion

I

of the examiner, but the first word of the group at which these older or brighter pupils commence should be written on the record sheet to enable the examiner later to calculate the score correctly.

Should a testee fail with any word of a group of ten words, when he has started at a point beyond the initial group of ten, then he should be taken back to read the preceding group of ten words.

*E.g.* A testee commencing at "smoulder" and failing on any word within this group should go back and read the group commencing "saucer." Care should be taken that all backward readers and dull pupils commence the test from the beginning.

All testees should continue with the test until they fail *in ten successive words.* This margin of failure (as each word in the test is more difficult than the preceding one) is sufficient with most pupils, but with older and brighter testees of 10+ onwards it is sometimes advisable, even after this limit of failure has been reached, to let them skim over the successive groups of words to see if there are any further words they recognise.

## CALCULATING READING AGE

The reading age is calculated from the total number of words correct. For example, here is the record sheet of Robina C., $9\frac{4}{12}$ :—

| tree | | | | |
|------|------|------|------|------|
| . | . | . | . | . |
| . | . | . | . | . |
| . | . | . | x | . |
| . | x | x | . | x |
| . | . | x | x | x |
| x | x | x | x | x |
| x | x | x | x | x |

Score, 23 words correct.

$$\text{Reading age} = \frac{\text{Number of words correctly read}}{10} + 5 \text{ years}$$

$$= \frac{23}{10} + 5 = 7\cdot3 \text{ years.}$$

Record sheet of John B., $10\frac{4}{12}$ :—

```
dream    .      .      .      ,
  .      .      .      ,
  .      .      .      x
  .      x      x      x
  .      x      x      x      .
  x      .      x      .      x
  .      x      x      x      x
  x      x      x      x      x
```

Score = 41 (21+20 words in 2 groups prior to " dream.")

Reading age $\frac{41}{10} + 5 = 9\cdot1$ years.

If an estimate of the pupil's reading ability in terms of chronological age is required, we can calculate the reading quotient.

$$\text{Reading quotient} = \frac{\text{Reading age}}{\text{Chronological age}} \times 100.$$

Thus John B.'s reading quotient $= \dfrac{9\cdot1}{10\frac{4}{12}} \times 100 = 88.$

(Remember that the reading ages are found in years and *tenths* of a year.)

# EXERCISES TO AID WORD DISCRIMINATION AND COMPREHENSION

THE exercises suggested below should be regarded simply as a supplementary means of assisting pupils in word discrimination and in phrase and sentence recognition. As I have indicated in foregoing chapters, specific word or phrase drill is no substitute for actual experience with meaningful reading material. The child learns to read most effectively if given full preparatory reading experiences, followed by frequent practice and adequate help with simple material. There is an immense gap between the exercise type of reading matter and the content of up-to-date reading books.

On the other hand there are many children in the initial stages of reading instruction, and later, a smaller group of less able pupils, who profit considerably by a little additional help with special aspects of learning to read. Exercises can be devised to assist their somewhat uncertain power of discriminating similar word patterns, e.g. of discriminating " stop " from " shop." The development of rapid phrase recognition and later, of phonic analysis, can also be aided. This help is most efficacious if the exercises are linked with such useful activities as drawing and colouring, and if they are so framed as to contain some of the elements of the game or the puzzle.

Reading exercises may be used as preparation or as revision for reading selected pages of a book, but they should never be allowed to replace the creative appeal of a centre of interest or the pleasure of dramatisation. Moreover, we should always remember that our final objective is

to give the child sufficient facility in the technique of reading to enable him quickly to understand what he is reading.
Hence the best kind of exercise is that which directs or tests
powers of comprehension. Here we should be ready, with
our most forward group of readers, to give them opportunity
for silent reading, motivated or checked by questions or
activities.

The exercises reproduced in the following pages are
merely samples of given types. There is no limit to the
examples an enthusiastic and ingenious teacher can construct
on these lines. Obviously the number and kind of such
exercises should be suited to the reading level of the pupils
and to the progress they are making. Some children do not
need to do such exercises, but nevertheless they enjoy the
fun of doing them quickly, especially those questions of
a game or puzzle kind.

## How to Use the Exercises

In the early stages of reading, the instructions for doing
the exercises should be read orally with the pupils. In
fact some of the exercises can be taken orally from the
blackboard; the teacher will readily recognise these
and will construct similar ones for the requirements of
particular groups of pupils. In the main, however, the
exercises are intended to be a means of linking up reading
with drawing and writing. For this purpose the class
teacher can trace off the line drawings given in the
book and can then reproduce copies of the drawings
and the exercise by means of some form of duplicating
machine. It is as well to remember when doing this to
run off extra sheets for another year's pupils. Additional
exercises can be constructed and prepared by the teacher,
as the single line drawings required do not demand a
very high level of artistic ability. The exercises can be

used a single sheet at a time, or can be made into a small booklet.[1]

## INTRODUCTORY BOOK (MATCHING CARDS)

A useful device in these early stages of reading for the slower and less able children is to provide them with dictionary or matching cards. These simply consist of small manilla cards, about the size of a playing card, on which is a picture of a character, object or activity which appears in their reading books. Under each picture is the correct word or phrase. The teacher also prepared slips of thin cardboard on which appear the names (words or phrases) only. The pupils may use (a) the cards with names on as dictionary cards, (b) the cards and the slips for matching one with the other.

[1] There is no need for this additional preparation for those using the *Happy Venture Readers*. Teachers can now procure the *Happy Venture Card Material* (Oliver and Boyd) which consists of sets of graded exercises to aid word recognition and comprehension. One set for each of the five *Happy Venture* books.

An explanatory note concerning the nature and use of the material for each book is given on pp. 121-147.

# SPECIMEN EXERCISES

THE EXERCISES ARE GRADED TO FIT IN WITH THE
APPROXIMATE ORDER OF PROGRESS IN READING
ABILITY.

Page 104. Matching cards.

Page 105. Drawing and colouring associated with words
and ideas in the reading book.

Page 106. Association of words with pictures; learning or
testing value.

Page 107. Association of sentences with pictures; learning
or testing value.

Page 108. Practice in recognition of phrases and sentences.

Page 109. Practice in word recognition through matching.

Page 110. Association of sentences and pictures; learning
or testing value.

Page 111. Word discrimination aided by recognition
through pictures.

Page 112. Word discrimination without the aid of pictures.

Page 113. Simple exercises in comprehension.

Page 114. Comprehension exercise.

Page 115. Exercises introducing pictures to aid early
stages of phonic analysis.

Page 116. Exercise to aid phonic analysis.

Page 117. Comprehension exercises.

MATCHING CARDS

DRAW A PICTURE OF NIP PLAYING WITH DICK

COLOUR THE PICTURES

This is Dora

Here is Nip

DRAW A LINE FROM THE WORD TO THE
PICTURE THAT GOES WITH IT

Fluff

Jane

Jack

tree

PUT A RING ROUND THE SENTENCE THAT
IS THE SAME AS THAT IN THE PICTURE

Mother has the ball.

Mother plays with Dick.

Mother has the ball.

Dora plays with Jane.

Dora has a doll.

Dora plays with Jane.

FIND THE LINE IN YOUR BOOK THAT SAYS:

> Jane is in the mud.
>
> Fluff is in the tree.
>
> Dora fell with the cat.

PUT A LINE IN GREEN CHALK UNDER 'BRING THE BALL.' PUT A LINE IN RED CHALK UNDER 'BY A TREE'

> Fluff is in the tree.
>
> The cat sits by a tree.
>
> Nip sits by a ball.
>
> Bring the ball.
>
> The ball is in a tree.
>
> Jack will bring the ball.
>
> The ball is by a tree.

DRAW A LINE UNDER THE WORDS IN THE SENTENCE
THAT LOOK JUST LIKE THE WORDS ON THE RIGHT

| | |
|---|---|
| Jack is in the tree. | the tree |
| Dora will bring Jane. | bring Jane |
| Nip sits with the ball. | Nip sits |
| Nip will play with Dick. | will play |

DRAW A PICTURE TO TELL US ABOUT THESE

| | |
|---|---|
| The ball stopped in the tree. | Nip brings the ball in his mouth. |

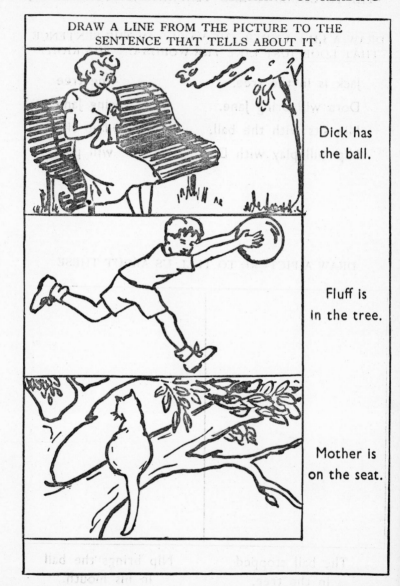

DRAW A LINE FROM THE PICTURE TO THE
SENTENCE THAT TELLS ABOUT IT

Dick has
the ball.

Fluff is
in the tree.

Mother is
on the seat.

DRAW A LINE UNDER THE WORD THAT
TELLS ABOUT THE PICTURE

| | |
|---|---|
| | ball<br><br>basket<br><br>dog |
| | basket<br><br>little<br><br>kitten |
| | sit<br><br>Nip<br><br>bit |
| | mud<br><br>tree<br><br>shoe |

## DRAW A LINE UNDER THE WORD THAT IS LIKE THE WORD IN THE BOX

shoe

| stop |

stop

see

basket

| basket |

ball

bad

for

| fun |

fat

fun

sat

| said |

said

saw

Draw these:                    a little kitten
                               a green basket
                               a big shoe
                               a rag doll

## WHO SAID?

DRAW A LINE TO THE ONE WHO SAID THESE:

"You cannot sit in the mud."        Fluff
                                     Mother

"I am wet with mud."                 Fluff
                                     Dick
                                     The Kitten

"I can hop on a line."               Nip
                                     Dick

"Bow wow, bow, wow."                 Jack
                                     Jane
                                     Nip

"My knee is cut."                    Dick
                                     Dora

K

## BLACKBOARD GAME
### PUT A RING ROUND THE RIGHT ANSWER

Dick is a boy.                          (Yes) or No

Jack is a girl.                          Yes or No

Dora sleeps in a basket.                Yes or No

The kitten is little.                   Yes or No

Nip sleeps in a shoe.                   Yes or No

Dick throws his bat at the ball.  Yes or No

Jack can hit the ball with his bat.  Yes or No

Dora skips well.                        Yes or No

You can wash a cat.                     Yes or No

You can wash a dog.                     Yes or No

A jumping jack is a toy.                Yes or No

Mother tied up Jack's knee with
    rag.                                Yes or No

## PHONIC PRACTICE
### PUT A RING ROUND THE WORD THAT TELLS ABOUT THE PICTURE

cat
hat
rat

fog
dog
log

sun
gun
run

hop
mop
top

big
dig
pig

hill
mill
pill

bed
led
red

sick
stick
Dick

DRAW A RING ROUND EACH WORD THAT ENDS
OR BEGINS LIKE THAT PART OF THE WORD
WITH A LINE UNDER IT IN THE BOX

| ba<u>ll</u> | t<u>op</u> | <u>sh</u>op |
|---|---|---|
| small | shop | shoe |
| nest | cut | bring |
| wall | skip | ship |
| sing | stop | stick |

| ri<u>ng</u> | we<u>ll</u> | <u>ta</u>ke |
|---|---|---|
| throw | tell | cake |
| bring | little | knee |
| line | fell | jump |
| jumping | small | make |

## QUESTIONS TO TEST COMPREHENSION
### (Pages 30, 31, Book I, HAPPY VENTURE READERS)

Who went to the shop ?

What can you see in the toy shop ?

Draw some of the toys you can see in the toy shop.

Draw the toy Dick got.

What can a jumping jack do ?

Draw what Dora got.

Who wanted a small ball ?

### (Pages 18 to 23, Book II, HAPPY VENTURE READERS)

## PUT IN THE WORDS LEFT OUT

Mother Hen has ———— chicks.

Little ———— Chick ran away.

"No, no, no," said Pig,
    "I must get my ————."

White Horse said :
    "I must go —— —— ——."

The Mother Hen found White Chick
    —— —— ——.

## COMPREHENSION EXERCISE

# DO YOU KNOW?

| | | |
|---|---|---|
| a saw | a potato | a horse |
| a table | a boot | an elephant |
| a clock | a broom | an armchair |
| a river | a match | a field of wheat |

1. What has arms but cannot move them?
2. Which has teeth but cannot chew?
3. Which has a face but does not wash it?
4. What has a mouth but cannot drink?
5. What has a head but cannot turn it?
6. What has hair but does not comb it?
7. Which has legs but cannot walk?
8. Which has eyes but cannot see?
9. What has a tongue but does not speak?
10. What has shoes but does not take them off?
11. What has ears but does not hear?
12. What has a trunk but does not pack his clothes in it?

COMPREHENSION EXERCISE

## PUZZLES

I have four legs.

I have a back.

I cannot walk.

People use me at table.

What am I?

I have wings.

I give light.

I come out at night.

I am very small.

What am I?

Sometimes I am small.

Sometimes I am tall.

I am not there at all if there is no sun.

What am I?

I like apples.

I like eggs.

I have brown eyes.

I have golden hair.

I am called Mar . . . . .

Who am I?

I have a head.

I have a foot.

I am not alive.

People use me at night.

What am I?

I can fly very fast.

I am pretty.

I can carry messages.

I sometimes save life.

What am I?

I shine brightly.

I guide men on their travels.

I cannot be seen when there is a lot of cloud.

What am I?

I can be used for cooking.

I come through pipes.

I am made from coal.

I give light.

What am I?

## PUZZLES (CONTINUED)

I have a handle.

I am made of iron.

I have a claw.

I make a noise when I work.

I am used by a carpenter.

What am I ?

I am made of glass.

I have a neck.

I hold all kinds of liquids.

I am closed by a stopper or a cork.

What am I ?

I am light.

I grow on a tree.

I float on water.

I am brown in colour.

What am I ?

I come from Africa.

I grow on trees.

I am gathered and sent to be crushed.

I am put in tins.

I am used to make something to drink.

What am I ?

I am made from soda and fat.

I smell nice.

I dissolve in water.

I am used to make things clean.

What am I ?

# EXERCISES IN CARD FORM BASED ON
## *THE HAPPY VENTURE READERS* [1]

IT will be clear to all those concerned with the teaching of reading that exercises such as those discussed in the previous section should serve two important purposes, firstly to speed up and consolidate pupils' powers of word recognition, and secondly, through this increased power, to enable them to read with increased speed and understanding. As an illustration of the card form of some of these exercises, and the uses to which they might be put, it will be pertinent to examine briefly the recently published card material for the *Happy Venture Readers*.[1] In the main the five sets of cards, one for each of the five books in the series, cover almost all of the exercises listed in page 103 except those for phonic analysis (pages 115 and 116).

## EXERCISES FOR INTRODUCTORY BOOK

### *Material*

(i) Set of 28 page-size picture cards. (ii) Set of 58 sentence strips. (iii) Set of single-word cards.

The total material consists of a set of 34 cards. There are 28 cards each the size of a page of the Introductory Book, a  d on the one side of each there is a coloured picture, similar to those in the book itself, accompanied by two

---

[1] *The Happy Venture Readers* Card Material, prepared by F. J. Schonell and G. Fleming. Introductory Set 3s., Set for Book One 2s. 6d., Set for Book Two 1s. 9d., Sets for Books Three and Four 1s. 6d. each. Available from Oliver and Boyd, Tweeddale Court, Edinburgh. Prices subject to alteration.

sentences in cards Nos. 1 to 26, and increased to three sentences in Nos. 27 and 28. On the reverse side of the card there is a picture alone to which pupils have to match the appropriate sentences. The sentences are printed on 58 strips for matching to each large card and its sentences— *e.g.*

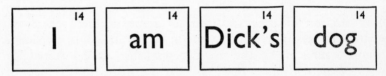

These are cut up and put in envelopes. In addition, the words of each sentence are printed on small cards—*e.g.*

| | | | |
|---|---|---|---|
| I | am | Dick's | dog |

These words pupils can build into the sentences, either to match to the sentences on picture and sentence cards, or to match to the sentence strip cards. In all cases the parent card and the appropriate word and sentence cards are numbered. Thus the method of using the material might be summarised in these steps.

(*a*) Present the card with the picture and accompanying sentences, *e.g.* (see page 123).

(*b*) Pupils place alongside or underneath the strips with the sentences to match. The matching of the sentences helps not only to strengthen word recognition, but to foster comprehension through the direct association of duplicate sentences with the picture (see page 124).

(*c*) Pupils select the appropriate sentences to go with the picture *alone* (see page 125).

# Here is Dick.

# Here is Nip.

(b)

Here is Dick.

Here is Dick.

Here is Nip.

Here is Nip.

(c)

Here is Dick.<sup>1</sup>

Here is Nip.<sup>1</sup>

(d) Pupils then build up sentences of separate words to match the sentences on the strips.

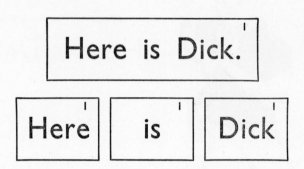

If pupils are slow in word recognition or have difficulty in selecting correct words to build up sentences, an additional step can be added, namely, building sentences from separate words to match the sentences on the picture plus sentence side of the card. (See Step (b).)

(e) A further step is to require pupils to build the correct sentences from the separate words.

Obviously in all this work the fact that each picture card with its appropriate sentence strips and word cards is similarly numbered, acts as a guide and a check to pupils. It is useful, so far as time and organisation permit, to encourage pupils to check their work with each other by reading aloud the sentences that have been matched.

Occasionally the teacher should take a section of slower readers and say to individual children, " Which is ' Nip ' ? " " Which is ' Here ' ? " " Hold up ' Nip.' " If this exercise is conducted with groups of pupils it leads to friendly and enthusiastic competition in ability to recognise the words separately. Children can also be placed in groups of four, five or six, each with a set of words, and shown how to play a game of snap with the words as they are revealed in turn.

## WRITING SENTENCES

Another exercise is for the teacher to use the sentence as flash cards with small groups of three or four children. All this practice recognition of words, phrases and sentences is an immense help when a pupil experiences the material in book form.

The exercises for both the Introductory Book and Book One may be used to link up writing and reading. There are some pupils whose powers of word recognition increase rapidly when their experience of words as visual patterns is reinforced by experience of them as movement (or writing) patterns. Thus it is sound pedagogical procedure to help some of the slower pupils to remember the patterns of words by encouraging them first to match the sentence and then to write it—slow, but often valuable in the early stages. In this way visual, auditory and kinæsthetic impressions of words are blended to reinforce each other.

## MAKING SENTENCES

After initial matching of all the sentences and building of the words into sentences to match the sentence strips has been completed, the pupil's word-recognition power can be further extended. He can be given a bag or envelope of the word cards for *making* sentences. A further exercise that appeals to some pupils illustrates how to make part of a sentence from the word cards and then to complete it with other different endings by selecting different word cards. Thus practice of this kind can be introduced :

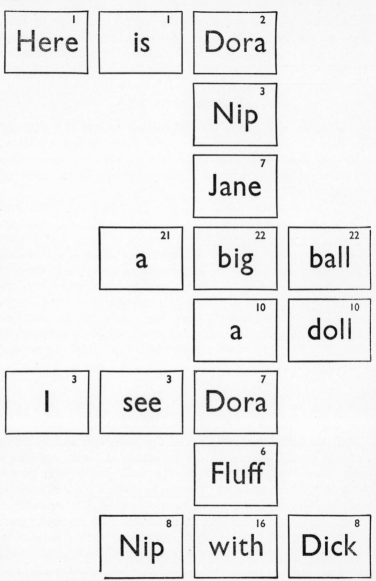

Here is Dora

Nip

Jane

a big ball

a doll

I see Dora

Fluff

Nip with Dick

It is apparent that card material provides teachers with the means of preparing all pupils in word and sentence recognition for reading the Introductory Book. At the same time it provides excellent practice for some pupils to consolidate through additional experience with words good habits of word or sentence recognition of which there might be evidence of weakness in the reading. The activity associated with this aspect of the reading instruction appeals strongly to pupils, and some of the less able readers make rapid strides through being able to " handle the words and sentences " in a material way. In matching the printed cards to pictures plus sentences, or to sentences alone, they are impelled to take stronger note of likenesses and differences and, at the same time, to pay attention to meaning through the association of sentences with the pictures.

Such matching exercises reach to the core of quick and successful word recognition. Classroom use of the cards reveals that children begin to realise the place of words as functional symbols in the sentence they are matching, or as brighter pupils soon see, in the new sentences they can build up from the words. In so far as the material is in card form it enables teachers to cater for individual needs or to plan effectively for group work.

## EXERCISES FOR BOOK ONE

### Material

(i) Set of 49 picture cards.
(ii) Set of 71 sentence strips.
(iii) Set of single-word cards from Card 12 onwards.

The material for Book One consists of 49 cards, 4″ × 3″, each with a coloured picture on it, *e.g.* a picture of Fluff, of Nip, Dora carrying Fluff, Dick running, and so on. To accompany these are sentence strip cards for matching to the picture cards. For the first nine exercises there are

L

27 picture cards, three picture cards to each exercise, and one sentence strip to be matched to each card. *e.g.*

5

## The kitten sits in the shoe.

For the remaining eleven exercises there are 22 picture cards, two picture cards to each exercise, and two sentence strips to be matched to each picture card. It will be observed that these exercises involve a step forward, for in this case the sentences do *not* appear *on* the pictures. The pupil omits the step of matching sentence to picture plus sentence and proceeds direct to matching sentences to pictures alone. For exercise 12 onwards there are single-word cards to build into sentences to match to the sentence strip cards, or into sentences related to the picture cards.

To introduce an element of variety, teachers can divide the 49 cards into seven sets allowing pupils to record their progress or to claim a mark, as each set is completed. The use of the cards in this way, as seven sets or seven units of work, thus enables each pupil to feel he has mastered something as he completes a unit.

## MAKING SENTENCES

As with the word-card material for the Introductory Book, pupils can be encouraged to build up new sentences from the words irrespective of the sentences on the strips. This not only assists reading but it is also a direct aid to English.

## EXERCISES FOR BOOK TWO

### Material

(i) Set of 17 cards for sentence building, for drawing and simple comprehension exercises.

(ii) Four sets of single-word cards to be cut up to make 218 word cards.

The material for this book takes the pupil a step further in the natural reading progress we are seeking to promote. In this set pictures are omitted. The pupil is expected at this stage to have achieved a certain level of word recognition. And for this reason the chief exercise to extend word recognition is the building of given sentences from single-word cards. The sentences are printed on each master card and the pupil builds these sentences from the numbered single-word cards. Again this exercise can be linked with writing. In addition, comprehension of sentences and puzzles is tested through the pleasurable exercise of drawing, and answers to questions by the selection of appropriate word cards.

## Exercises for Book Three

### Material

    (i) 15 sets of cards, comprehension exercises.
   (ii) 51 sentence strips to be used for answering exercises.
  (iii) 33 phrase and word cards for answering exercises.

The purpose of the exercises at this level is to develop and check powers of comprehension. Coincident with practice in mastering the mechanics of reading, *i.e.*, word recognition, pupils should receive definite help in developing quick and accurate understanding of what they read. This is best achieved in the early stages of learning to read through a variety of exercises that demand a minimum of actual writing. Hence the exercises for Books Three and Four require answers to questions of the " who," " where," " what " kind, not by writing, but by selecting the correct sentence strip.

Every exercise is numbered and lettered so that all the pupils need to do is to place the number and letter on the left-hand side of their answer paper, and then lay alongside it the correct sentence strip, phrase or word strip. Thus the answers to the first part of Card I would appear as follows :—

---

I

# GOING TO SCHOOL

A 1. Who are going to school?

   2. Whom did they meet?

   3. What did Jack take to school?

   4. What did Jess take to school?

---

A 1. | Dick and Dora are going to school. | IA

2. | They met Jack and Jess. | IA

3. | Jack took his kite. | IA

4. | Jess took her doll. | IA

Alternatively of course, pupils may be required to place the answer strip alongside each of the questions on the answer card, but an introduction to the numbering of answers is useful practice for a situation that will soon occur many times in their school work. There is little point in requiring pupils to write out the actual questions asked since this would greatly impede the amount of reading, and the object of the exercises is to give practice in comprehension.

The exercises include questions, puzzles (What am I? Who am I?), drawing, writing out a list of articles from a story, and supplying missing words.

### Exercises for Book Four

#### *Material*

(i) 12 sets of card comprehension exercises.
(ii) 73 sentence strips to be used for answering exercises.
(iii) 25 word cards for answering exercises.

As with the comprehension exercises for Book Three, pupils are required to answer questions and puzzles, supply missing words, etc., by selecting the appropriate sentence strip or word card. At this stage the exercises introduce a little more writing—pupils write out complete sentences and also write short stories.

## MATCHING SENTENCES USED FOR BOOK ONE

These sentences have to be matched to the forty-nine picture cards. Then the separate words should be built into these sentences.

### *One sentence to each picture*

Card 1. Fluff is a big cat.
Fluff runs to her basket.
This is Fluff's basket.

Card 2. Here is Nip.
Nip is with the kitten.
Nip runs.

Card 3. It is Fluff's kitten.
The kitten plays with the ball.
The little kitten can run.

Card 4. You bad dog, Nip !
Dora takes the kitten.
Nip and the kitten run.

Card 5. The bad kitten is in the mud.
Fluff washes the kitten.
The kitten sits in the shoe.

Card 6. Dora hops on the line.
Dick runs.
Here are Dick and Dora.

Card 7. Dora ran to the tree.
Dick fell in the mud.
Dick and Dora hop on the line.

Card 8. Dick can hop.
Jack can jump.
Dora can run.

Card 9. One little kitten sits by the tree.
Two little kittens sit by the tree.
One little kitten runs up the tree.

*Two sentences to each picture*

Card 10. Jack has the ball.
He throws the ball.
Dick has the bat.
He hits the ball.

Card 11. Dick has hit the ball.
He has one run.
Dora has the ball.
She throws it to Jack.

Card 12. Jack can jump well.
He will jump, one, two, three.
May can skip well.
She will skip, one, two, three.

Card 13. Dick said, "I can hop well."
Dick will hop, hop, hop.
Dora said, "I can run well."
Dora will run, run, run.

Card 14. Dora has her doll, Jane.
Jane sits in Fluff's basket.
May sits on a seat.
The seat is by the tree.

Card 15. Dora can wash Jane.
She is a rag doll.
Nip jumps up to the rag doll.
He is a bad, bad dog.

Card 16. Jack can not skip well.
He fell and cut his knee.
Mother tied up Jack's knee.
She tied it with a bit of rag.

Card 17. Mother sits on the seat.
Fluff is with Mother.
Nip is with May.
"Bow-wow, Bow-wow," said Nip.

Card 18. Dora and May are with Mother.
They go to the toy shop.
This is a toy shop.
Do you see all the toys?

Card 19. Dick likes the jumping jack.
It can go jump, jump, jump.

Dick said, "I will get a big bat."
Dora said "I will get a big doll."

Card 20. The little kitten is here with Fluff.
Nip plays with Fluff's kitten.
May plays with Dora.
They wash the rag doll.

## MATCHING SENTENCES USED FOR BOOK TWO

### SENTENCES AS THEY APPEAR IN ORDER ON CERTAIN CARDS

These sentences have to be matched from the words provided. All other sentences on the cards relate only to drawing or writing instructions. Some cards have no sentences for matching, but have only drawing exercises or puzzles to test comprehension.

Card 1 A. There are two little rabbits.
One rabbit is for you.

Card 2 C. My toy can go jump, jump.
The cat and dog can run.

Card 3 A. Jack has tea with Dick.
Dick will bring three eggs.

Card 4 A. Nip is with three little kittens.
One kitten is in the basket.

B. Dora put the hat on Nip.
May put rag on the kitten.

Card 8 A. I have a little white kite.
The kite has a big string.

B. My white kite can fly high.
See it go up and up.

Card 9 C. Little White Chick is a bad chick.
Five chicks find White Chick in a tree.

Card 10 A. Four children went to the park.
They had tea by the big tree.

B. The children play in a ring.
They hold hands and sing.

Card 11 B. I was hopping and hit my nose.
I was jumping and cut my leg.

C. Mother tied up one rabbit's eye.
She tied up one rabbit's ear.

Card 13   Four children made shadows on the wall.
Can you make funny shadows ?

Card 14 A. Two little pigs were bad pigs.
One little pig was a good pig.

B. A big dog saw two pigs.
They ran home so fast.

Card 16 A. Six children make a ring.
They hold hands and sing.

B. Five children dance and sing.
They are all in a ring.

Card 17 D. The monkey had Dora's hat in his hand.
They had a ride on the big elephant.


## ANSWERS TO QUESTIONS

The following lists will serve as a handy guide to the teachers in checking sentences and answers.


### Book Three

CARD 1            GOING TO SCHOOL

A 1. Dick and Dora are going to school.
  2. They met Jack and Jess.
  3. Jack took his kite.
  4. Jess took her doll.

B 1. Dick has a book like Jack's.
  2. Jack and Dick read well.
  3. The first story was "The Three Little Pigs."
  4. Dora read the story.


CARD 2            THE THREE LITTLE PIGS

A 1. The first little pig had straw.
  2. The second little pig had sticks.
  3. The third little pig had bricks.
  4. The wolf blew down two houses.

B 1. He went for turnips at five o'clock.
  2. He went for apples at four o'clock.
  3. He went to the fair at two o'clock.

C   The third little pig.

CARD 3           **DINNER TIME**

A 1. Dora set the table for dinner.
   2. Dick got some water for Nip.
   3. Father did Rat-a-tat-tat on the **door.**
   4. Mother cut the pudding.

B     A knife.

CARD 4          **THE FUNNY MONKEY**

A 1. Jess read this story.
   2. Monkey went to see Rabbit.
   3. They went to see Nip.
   4. Each one had some pudding.

B 1. Rabbit ran best.
   2. Nip danced best.
   3. Monkey did the best trick.
   4. The pudding was the prize.

CARD 5          **THE BIG ENGINE**

A 1. Dick and Dora went with father.
   2. Dick wanted to see the engine.
   3. The two men were the driver and the fireman.
   4. The big engine needs coal and water.

B 1. The fire turns the water into steam.
   2. The steam makes the engine go.
   3. The engine has big wheels and small wheels.
   4. The wheels run on steel lines.

CARD 6    THE LITTLE COAL TRUCK

A I. The little coal truck waited at the station.
2. The coal was wanted over the hill.
3. The little engine puffed slowly up the hill.
4. It went faster down the hill.

B I. Little coal truck.
2. Little engine.
3. Smaller engine.
4. Big engine.

CARD 7            SHOPPING

B I. grocer's shop.
2. Mr Brown.
3. three pounds.
4. six eggs.

CARD 8        BAKING DAY

I. Dick.                3. Mother.
2. Dora.                4. The cake.

CARD 9        THE PARTY

A I. The party was on Saturday afternoon.
2. Dora asked Jess and May.
3. Dick asked George and Jack.
4. They put the letters in the post box.

B I. four.               3. six.
2. seven.             4. three.

## THE BROWN MOUSE AND THE CLOCK

CARD 10

A. There are no word cards for this exercise. The following words, which pupils write, should be considered as correct answers :—

A 1. eyes or ears.
   2. head or tail or nose or mouth or body.
   3. feet or legs.

B 1. two.
   2. Brown mouse.
   3. Black mouse.
   4. nut.
   5. wanted.

CARD 11     THE LOST SHOE

A 1. smith.
   2. miller.
   3. shopman.
   4. farmer.
   5. miner.

CARD 12     THE TAR BABY

A 1. Mr Fox had a fine garden.
   2. White Tail was eating the carrots.
   3. Mr Fox wanted to catch White Tail.
   4. It was made of sticks and black tar.

CARD 13     AT THE FIRE STATION

A 1. Dick first saw the fire.
   2. Dick's father sent a call to the fire station.
   3. A wire was inside the red box.
   4. A bell would ring at the fire station.

B 1. fire-engine.
   2. hose.
   3. fire.
   4. helmets.

## ANSWERS TO QUESTIONS FOR BOOK FOUR

CARD 1  OFF FOR THE HOLIDAYS

A 1. They were going to the seaside.
   2. Four cases were packed.
   3. They started at 10 o'clock.
   4. He asked for four return tickets to Seatown.

B 1. cows ; horses.
   2. soldiers.
   3. twelve.
   4. half.

CARD 2  AT THE SEASIDE

A 1. Mother told them to go to the beach.
   2. Dick wanted to make a fort.
   3. They put in shells for windows.
   4. They dug a moat round the fort.

B 1. early.         4. shell.
   2. beach.       5. fly.
   3. tide.        6. oil.

CARD 3  THE MERRY-GO-ROUND

   1. Three children went down.
   2. They saw a Merry-Go-Round.
   3. They each paid a penny for a ride.
   4. Mother gave them the pennies.

CARD 4        BOMBO THE ELEPHANT

A 1. Uncle told the story.
  2. Bombo was his name.
  3. Kip looked after Bombo.
  4. Bombo piled up heavy logs.
  5. Bombo liked to swim in the river.

B 1. A tailor makes clothes.
  2. He gave Bombo a bun.
  3. He pricked Bombo's trunk with a pin.
  4. Bombo squirted dirty water over him.

C    An elephant.

CARD 5        HOW DICK AND MALCOLM
           SAW THE CIRCUS

A 1. Dora went with Mother and Auntie to the shops.
  2. They went to see men getting ready for the circus.
  3. Dick and Malcolm took water to the elephants.
  4. There were eight ponies.

B 1. The first man gave them the tickets.
  2. The circus started at eight o'clock.
  3. The ponies could stand on their hind legs.
  4. The elephant and two clowns sat on the see-saw.

C    A seal.

CARD 6    THE NASTURTIUMS THAT WERE
        TOO PROUD FOR THEIR BOOTS

A 1. Roderick read the story.
  2. Dick, Dora and Malcolm listened.

   3. They were planted in a pair of old boots.
   4. Ben got the soil from his friend's garden.

B 1. The plants grew very tall.
   2. The flowers were red, gold, yellow and orange.
   3. The baker thought Ben's house was on fire.
   4. He picked up a bucket of water and ran down
      the road.

CARD 7      JOEY, THE KANGAROO

A 1. Malcolm told this story.
   2. Kangaroos live in Australia.
   3. Baby Kangaroo lived in a warm pocket of fur.
   4. They liked to eat nice green grass.

B 1. Kangaroos hop.
   2. Dogs run.
   3. The kangaroos won the race.
   4. She had left him in a large bush.
   5. He jumped in with one big hop.

CARD 8      WE SEE THE SHIPS

A 1. Seven people were going to see the ships.
   2. They took a picnic lunch with them.
   3. They went by bus.
   4. Each ticket cost fourpence.

B 1. Dora saw red, orange, yellow, and green funnels.
   2. They saw eight big ships.
   3. There were four cranes working.
   4. One ship brought butter from Australia.

M

CARD 9      DOWN GOES A LIFEBOAT

A 1. The painters fell into the sea.
  2. The officer ordered the lifeboat out.
  3. There were eight sailors in the lifeboat.
  4. The lifeboat was lowered by strong ropes.

B 1. tugs.
  2. slowly.
  3. lighthouse.
  4. sea-gull.
  5. gangway ; cranes.

CARD 10      THE PICNIC

A 1. The red bus took them near the fields.
  2. Malcolm got the tickets.
  3. They left the bus at twenty minutes past one o'clock.
  4. Roderick found a good place for the picnic.

B 1. Uncle knew how to light a fire.
  2. Uncle made a hole in the ground.
  3. They needed small dry stick, paper and big sticks.

C 1. A match was used to light the fire.
  2. They had made a camp fire.
  3. They had to see that the fire was out.

CARD 11      GOOD-BYE SEATOWN

A 1. Dora.
   2. Roderick.
   3. Malcolm.
   4. Dick.

B 1. long ; home.
   2. dry ; fine.
   3. Dick ; Dora.
   4. Malcolm ; Roderick.


CARD 12      THE LAST DAY OF THE HOLIDAYS

A 1. Father took them to the Zoo.
   2. They wanted to see the panda.
   3. Dick took some nuts for the monkeys.
   4. May went with them to the Zoo.
   5. The keeper showed them the way.

# METHODS AND MATERIALS FOR BACKWARD READERS IN THE SENIOR SCHOOL

PUPILS who enter the Senior School unable to read are usually boys who have, from the earliest stages of reading instruction, been handicapped by a specific mental weakness in the ability of learning to read. Sometimes this special mental disability has been accentuated by the additional one of dullness, or subnormality in general intelligence, while in not a few cases numerous absences from school have further handicapped pupils already unable to make normal progress in school.

With some of these backward boys the junior school has made most persistent efforts to teach them to read; with others their continued failure is in no small measure due to ineffective and insufficient reading instruction in junior classes. Teachers of these older backward children are thus faced with a difficult psychological-educational problem of which they must understand the elements before they can plan methods and materials.

## FOUR FUNDAMENTALS

There are four fundamental points which should be carefully considered when planning the reading lessons for these backward readers.

(1) Most of these pupils of 11 or 12, although backward in school work, have the outlook and interests of the average boy of 11 or 12. They do the same things, play the same games and are interested in the same topics. Although their reading age may be only 7 or 8 years yet they differ very much in their understanding, speech and interests from the 7- or 8-year-old boy. *This means that somehow we must use reading*

*material, sufficiently simplified, suited to the interests, activities and conversation of average* 11- *or* 12-*year-old children.*

(2) These pupils represent a residue of really difficult cases of reading disability, where specific mental handicaps, sometimes accentuated by general intellectual weakness, have rendered progress by ordinary methods of reading instruction almost impossible. It is therefore necessary to make a specialised scientific approach to their difficulties, and *to use modern diagnostic measures to find out the causes for their continued failure.*

(3) Nearly all backward readers in the Senior School have failed for 6 or 7 years with the usual methods of teaching reading as generally used in infant and junior school classes. It is therefore useless to continue with the same kind of instruction now that these pupils have entered a new department or have come under the care of a different teacher. *We must devise a new approach which will, at least in the initial stages, have novelty and ensure immediate success.*

(4) Because these pupils have failed for so long, and because the consequences of their failure have been so apparent to them and to others, they have lost confidence in themselves and failed to maintain normal self-esteem. Differently with different children this has resulted in apathy or boredom, and a longing to be free of the whole atmosphere of school and scholastic failure. With others it has resulted in fierce antagonism towards a system which so condemns and perpetuates their disability—there are things they *can* do, but so seldom are they given a chance to show this. Others of these handicapped children have sought compensatory satisfaction in anti-social behaviour and even in delinquency. Therefore the reading programme for backward readers must be intimately linked with a reorientation of their whole school programme. They must be provided with plenty of opportunity for expressing themselves and thus regaining their lost self-esteem and diminished self-confidence. *That is, not only their reading lessons but the whole of their school work must be*

*planned along therapeutic lines.* The reading must be woven skilfully into other activities, and these must be activities which they like, and which they can do. Doing and learning must be not merely a catch phrase but a dominant character-istic of their curriculum. Now, all this is best done through a *small special class*, where special methods with plenty of sympathetic consideration can be given to each individual. Personally, I believe it is almost impossible to make much progress with these very backward children in an ordinary class with the usual senior school syllabus and time-table.

## PLANNING THE METHOD

In planning the method there are again four important aspects of the problem which should be covered.

(1) The teachers should *accurately determine each boy's reading age.* This is probably best done by giving the graded reading test as set out on pages 92-93. This will immedi-ately give the teacher a fairly accurate idea of the amount of reading backwardness present, and of the vocabulary level of material that the boy can be expected to attempt.

(2) This step should be followed by an *application of a number of diagnostic reading tests.* The teacher can obtain help here from Chapter VIII, *Backwardness in the Basic Subjects*, in which details are given of a simple diagnostic testing programme together with diagnostic tests (Appendix III, *Backwardness in the Basic Subjects*, Oliver and Boyd).

(3) The next step is to *introduce the boys to a method which will be different* from the type of reading lesson they have usually had, and which will therefore not suffer from the negative effects of past reading failure. Here again I have outlined elsewhere in some detail what I have found to be a useful approach. (*Backwardness in the Basic Subjects*, pages 216-220 and pages 244-247.) Teachers may also like to acquaint themselves with a slightly modified form of the

methods advocated above. These were tried out by W. V. Warmington in " C " classes of a large Senior School, and are outlined in *The Teacher's Companion* to "The New Vista Readers" (Schofield & Sims).

It is essential with backward readers to give, where possible, two short lessons per day. The gain in reading attainment, the consequent improvement in other school work and, above all, the resulting improvement in personality adjustment and development make this fully worth while.

(4) Once the pupils are making some progress with the special method, it is necessary to introduce them to *text-books specially suited* to their limited but particular type of reading ability.

The following are a list of books which senior boys like and can use as they begin to make reading progress. These are roughly graded from a reading age of 7 upwards :—

*Happy Venture Readers*, Book IV (Oliver and Boyd). Has a controlled vocabulary and contains much of interest to 11-year-olds.

*The First and Second School Story Books* (Nelson). Based to some extent on the picture strip method, the material in these books is useful for backward boys.

*The Speedwell Book* (Cassell & Co.). Worked out in a special school with very backward readers.

*The New Vista Readers* (Schofield & Sims). Good clear type and illustrations. Worked out with C Classes in a Senior School.

*The Escalator Individual Reading Booklets* (Oliver and Boyd Ltd.). Fifteen carefully graded small booklets, each containing two short stories, and suitable for backward senior pupils with reading ages ranging from 6 to 9+ years. The booklets are arranged in three series and the careful grading of the material from a R.A. of 6+ onwards, together with a systematic provision for phonic work render them effective with older pupils needing quick success. Comprehension exercises in Teacher's Manual.

*The Pathfinder Books* (Oliver and Boyd Ltd.). A series of three books with controlled vocabularies. Interesting material and illustrations to suit senior pupils. Teachers will find these very helpful class text-books in so far as they blend instruction in reading, spelling and written English in a natural way.

*Read, Laugh and Learn* (Grant Educational Co.). These contain short stories with an element of humour and are popular with backward pupils.

*The New Foundation Readers* (University of London Press). Controlled vocabulary. Simple stories with short sentences.

*A Book of Interests* (Nisbet). Well illustrated, good selection of material.

" The Active Readers "—*La Bonte, X Bar Y Ranch, White Hawk* (Ginn & Co.).

These are fine books with excellent illustrations and interesting exercises on each chapter. I have found that most backward readers, once their reading age reaches the 8-year level, develop through these books the desire and the power to read by themselves.

*The Wide Range Readers* (F. Schonell and P. Flowerdew) have been especially planned to cater for the wide range in reading attainments of pupils between the ages of 7 and 11. These books are graded by control of vocabulary and sentence structure, *according to reading age*, and are in two parallel series, each of six books. Books I to IV are graded by half-yearly reading ages and hence allow of their use with sections or groups of pupils within each class. The scheme is as follows :—

Blue Book    I and Green Book    I.    Reading age  7 -7½
Blue Book   II and Green Book   II.    Reading age  7½-8
Blue Book  III and Green Book  III.    Reading age  8 -8½
Blue Book   IV and Green Book   IV.    Reading age  8½-9
Blue Book    V and Green Book    V.    Reading age  9-10
Blue Book   VI and Green Book   VI.    Reading age  10-11+

Books I to IV, both series, will be found to be of particular value with backward readers between the ages of 7 and 12+.

When further progress has been made it is a good plan to introduce the pupils to short simplified forms of well-known books as found, for example, in the " New Method Readers " (Longmans). This can be followed by an introduction to longer books of certain authors—always remember to suit the material to the reading age. Thus some boys will be able to read by themselves the books by A. Ransome (*Swallows and Amazons*, *The Big Six*, *Coot Club*, etc.). Some of my backward readers, both boys and girls, made amazing progress once they had commenced these books.

# INDEX

Abilities, special, 17, 19, 20, 27, 78
Activities, reading, 15, 16, 24, 42, 49, 53
  school, 31, 34, 45, 55, 122
Age group, 44
Analysis of words, 14, 19, 23, 24, 47, 61, 73, 75, 96
  of reading methods, 44-65
Aptitudes, specific, 19, 23, 45
Association, of letters, 23
Auditory recognition, 14, 15, 17, 20, 23
  power, 27

Backwardness, 23, 70, 78, 123
Backward readers, 13, 50, 75, 78, 80, 83, 85, 95, 148-152
Bloomster, M., 46
Buhler, C., 31
Boyce, E., 31

Calendar, nature, 41
Cards, matching, 40, 41, 72, 102
  picture, 48, 76
Children, dull, 18, 19, 26, 28, 47, 49, 50, 64, 66, 95, 148
  intelligent, 18, 26, 27, 31, 41, 59, 66, 80, 98
  mentally defective, 18, 27
  nervous, 95, 97
  Scottish, 16
  unstable, 27
Class, organisation of reading, 66, 78-89, 149-151
  sections in, 22, 28, 47, 60, 83
  special, 150
Colouring, 35, 40
Competition, 67
Composition, 79
Confidence, 17, 25, 26, 47, 58, 59-67, 94, 97, 149
Copying, 12, 17, 40, 41
Correlations, 18
Curriculum, 16, 88

Defects, sensory, 19, 29
Delinquency, 79, 149
Development, rates of, 25, 26, 67
Diagnostic testing, 80, 86, 149

Discrimination of word patterns, 11, 12, 13, 17, 19, 20, 23, 24, 48, 50, 61, 100
Dolch, E. W., 46
Dramatisation, 56, 100
Drawing, 17, 31, 32, 34, 38, 100, 101, 103
Drill, 57, 59, 71

Emotional attitudes, 17, 19, 24, 26, 27, 29
Experiences, child, 24, 25, 26, 27, 29, 33, 35, 40, 42, 50, 53, 88
  pre-reading, 30, 100
Eye units, 23

Factors, educational, 19
  environmental, 17, 24, 53
  in reading, 17, 18, 26, 53
  physiological, 19
  psychological, 11-25, 27
Failure, 25, 26, 49, 71, 98, 149
Fletcher, C., 88
Folk tales, 54

Games, 68
Gardner, D. E. M., 66
Grading, of material, 57, 58, 60
Group, methods, 67, 72, 84
  study, 34, 40, 41, 53, 88
Guessing, 49, 97

Hayes, A. E., 45
Hearing, power of, 19
Home conditions, 26, 68
Hume, G. E., 31

Ideas, word, 17
Illiteracy, 79, 85
Illustrations, book, 49, 50, 60, 72
Individual methods, 67, 72, 84, 150
Infant readers, 16, 20
  schools, 15, 26, 28, 30, 66, 78, 79, 149
Intelligence, general, 17, 18, 19, 27, 28, 73, 78
  quotient, 18, 27, 28, 29
  tests, 28

Interest, 17, 25, 33, 45, 49, 53, 54, 88
  Centre of, 16, 34, 35, 50, 53, 56, 66, 68
Interests of children, 88, 89, 148

Jenkinson, A. J., 89
Jensen, M., 19
Junior classes, 78-89, 148, 149

Kinæsthetic impressions, 17
Knox, R. B., 34

Language, background, 15, 17, 19, 24, 26, 27, 43, 63, 67, 86, 88
  experience, 16, 20
Length of words, 12
Letters, in words, 13
  confusion of, 27
Look and Say Method, see Word Whole
Libraries, 88, 89

Matching, words, 49, 52, 70, 102
  sentences, 49, 52, 70, 72
Maturation, 19, 23, 25, 28, 78
Meaning of words, 12, 15, 24, 50, 63, 74
Memory, 24, 57
Mental age, 18, 19, 24, 28, 29, 44, 47, 61, 64
Methods, teaching, 25, 26

Nursery, classes, 32, 66
  school, 30

Objectives, in reading, 88, 89, 100

Painting, 17, 32, 34, 35, 100
Parental attitudes, 25, 31
Patterns, visual, 11, 12, 19, 20, 45, 57, 63
  word, 13, 16, 19, 24
Perception, 18, 19, 20, 23, 26, 27
Persistence, 25, 27, 70
Personality, 26, 79, 151
Phonic analysis, 103
  lists, 74, 75
  methods, 14, 15, 44-48, 52, 61, 72-76
  units, 24
Phonoscript method, 45
Pictures, 15, 24, 31, 35, 41, 45, 48, 49, 60, 66, 69, 103

Play, 15, 17, 20, 29, 30, 31, 33, 34, 35, 53
Preparatory stage in reading, 15, 19, 25, 26-43
Print, 20, 94
  arrangement of, 22
Projects, 20, 47, 53, 66, 68
Pronunciation, 24, 63, 97

Reading, ability, 17, 24, 25, 26, 27
  ages, 21, 22, 82, 83, 84, 86, 98, 99, 150
  attainments, 79, 80-83
  comprehension, 18, 22, 47, 61, 77, 101, 103
  errors, 24
  exercises, 41, 100-120
  eye movements, 21, 22, 23, 47
  lessons, 18, 19, 26, 43, 44, 66, 70, 82, 151
  modern development in teaching, 53-65
  preparation for, 15, 19, 25, 26-43, 49, 68
  reactions, early, 11, 12
  readiness, 18, 19, 28, 29, 41
  sheets, 35, 38, 40, 41
  silent, 72, 77, 80, 83, 84, 87
  speed of, 22, 72, 81
  tests, 77, 80, 85, 87, 90-99, 150
  units, 47, 48, 49, 61
Recognition, of phrases, 103
  of words, 13, 14, 18, 21, 24, 32, 39, 82
  span of, 22
Relationships, 18
Reliability ratio, 85
Research, 19, 26, 46, 58, 83
  Scottish Council for, 16, 58
Rhymes, 15, 33, 41, 42, 75, 76, 77
Rhythm, 56, 87

Schonell, F. J., 23, 77, 78, 84, 150
Senior schools, 84, 148-152
Sensory powers, 19
Sentence, length of, 20, 50, 55, 74
Sentence Method, 44, 49-52, 67, 70
Serjeant, F. I., 31, 32, 42
Sheets, cyclostyled, 40
Sight, power of, 19
Smith, C. A., 19
Sounds of, consonants, 47, 76, 77
  letters, 45, 46, 64
  vowels, 45, 65, 74, 77

Space, eye, 21, 23
Span of recognition, 22
Speech, 31, 32
  direct, 56
Spelling, 79
Stevens, M. P., 34
Stories, 15, 24, 32, 38, 46, 53, 54,
  56, 66, 74, 84

Teachers, 26, 44, 47, 48, 49, 53, 54,
  86
Terman Merrill Intelligence Test,
  28
Tests, *see* Reading tests
Time tables, 41, 150
Tracing impressions, 12, 16, 17, 71,
  86
Training Colleges, 79
Transfer of knowledge, 75
Type, size of, 20, 21, 82

Units, reading, *see* Reading

Vernon, A. C., 16
Vernon, P. E., 16
Vocabulary, child's, 16, 24, 27, 29,
  31, 39, 40, 42, 45, 86
  reading, 15, 50, 56, 60, 70, 71
Vowels, *see* Sounds of letters

Warmington, W. V., 150
Weather charts, 41
Word lists, 60, 71
Word Whole Method, 44, 45, 47,
  48, 49, 52, 67, 70
Words, confusion of, 46
  common, 16, 40, 46, 53, 63, 75, 82
  irregular, 45, 47, 48
  new per page, 57, 58
  regular, 45
  repetition of, 56, 59
Word books, 40, 52, 72, 101
Writing, 12, 16, 32, 41, 52, 86,
  101

PRINTED IN GREAT BRITAIN BY OLIVER AND BOYD LTD., EDINBURGH